BOOK OF SECRETS: ANCIENT SECRETS

KEN HUDNALL
OMEA PRESS
EL PASO, TEXAS 79912

BOOK OF SECRETS: ANCIENT SECRETS

COPYRIGHT © 2017 KEN HUDNALL

All rights reserved. No part of the book may be reproduced or transmitted in any form or by any means, graphic, electronic, or mechanical, including photocopying, recording, taping or by any information storage or retrieval system, without the permission in writing of the author.

OMEGA PRESS

http://www.kenhudnall.com

FIRST EDITION

Printed in the United States of America

OTHER WORKS BY THE SAME AUTHOR UNDER THE NAME KEN HUDNALL FROM OMEGA PRESS

MANHATTAN CONSPIRACY SERIES
Blood on the Apple
Capitol Crimes
Angel of Death
Confrontation

THE OCCULT CONNECTION
UFOs, Secret Societies and Ancient Gods
The Hidden Race
Flying Saucers
UFOs and the Supernatural
UFOs and Secret Societies
UFOs and Ancient Gods
Evidence of Alien Contact
Intervention
Secrets of Dulce
Unidentified Flying Objects
Sensual Alien Encounters
Strange Creatures From Time and Space
Introduction to Roswell
Alien Encounters
Mysteries of Space
Battle of Los Angeles

DARKNESS
When Darkness Falls
Fear the Darkness

SPIRITS OF THE BORDER
(with Connie Wang)
The History and Mystery of El Paso Del Norte
The History and Mystery of Fort Bliss, Texas

(with Sharon Hudnall)
The History and Mystery of the Rio Grande
The History and Mystery of New Mexico
The History and Mystery of the Lone Star State
The History and Mystery of Arizona
The History and Mystery of Tombstone, AZ
The History and Mystery of Colorado
Echoes of the Past
El Paso: A City of Secrets
Tales From the Nightshift
The History and Mystery of Sin City
The History and Mystery of Concordia
The History and Mystery of ASARCO
Military Ghosts
School Spirits
Restless spirits
Railroad Ghosts
Nautical Ghosts
Haunted Hotels
Haunted Hotels in Arizona and Colorado
Ghosts of Albuquerque
The History and Mystery of Tucson
The History and Mystery of Santa Fe

SHADOW WARS
The Shadow Rulers
The Secret Elite

THE ESTATE SALE MURDERS
Dead Man's Diary

A Bloody Afternoon of Fun

Northwood Conspiracy

No Safe Haven: Homeland Insecurity

Where No Car Has Gone Before

Seventy Years and No Losses: The History of the Sun Bowl

How Not To Get Published

Lost Cities and Hidden Tunnels Along the Border

Vampires, Werewolves and Things That Go Bump in The Night

Border Escapades of Billy the Kid

Criminal law for the Layman

Understanding Business Law

Language of the Law

Death of Innocence: The Life and Death of Vince Foster

The Veterans' Practice Primer

PUBLISHED BY PAJA BOOKS
The Occult Connection: Unidentified Flying Objects

PUBLISHED BY PRUNE DANISH PRESS
Why Would They Say It?

DEDICATION

As with all of my endeavors, this would not be possible without the support and assistance of my lovely wife, Sharon Hudnall.

TABLE OF CONTENTS

TABLE OF CONTENTS	9
WHAT ARE ANCIENT SECRETS?	11
COULD THE BIBLE BE CORRECT?	25
A GIFT OF THE GODS	37
HOW OLD IS CIVILIZATION ON EARTH?	59
THERE WERE GIANTS IN THOSE DAYS	77
MORE EVIDENCE THAT THERE WERE GIANTS IN THOSE DAYS	91
STRANGE CREATURES FROM TIME AND SPACE	107
HUMANITY'S INHUMAN GUIDES	123
OTHER MYSTERIOUS CREATURES	137
INDEX	151

CHAPTER ONE

WHAT ARE ANCIENT SECRETS?

In a volume such as this, it is first necessary to define exactly what we are discussing. In using the term ancient secrets we are talking about technology and discoveries from the distant past that are either being rediscovered or reinvented today. As a result of the discovery of some of these ancient secrets, it is necessary to re-evaluate out beliefs about the primitive nature of our ancestors.

Granted, we believe that out civilization is the epitome of scientific advancement just as we believe that the further back in time you go, the more primitive society and man becomes. However, let us suppose that this premise, which frankly is taught in school, is not only not true, but in some cases an intentional façade to divert research that would result in discoveries that would detrimentally effect economic interests today and actually destroy many academic careers.

Of course, at this point, I know that many readers are shaking their heads slowly, believing that the writer is getting ready to take flight into a fantasy world of make believe and supposition. However, what would happen to the reader's preconceived notions of how the world and history progressed if it could be shown that there is actual proof, granted, some of it circumstantial, that what we are taught about history is not true?

It should be remembered that history is written by the winners (or the most powerful), not necessarily the most truthful. It should also be remembered that usually long dead leaders in the various academic fields write history and, over time, their writings become dogma not subject to examination or contradiction. This is especially true in the field of archeology upon which much ancient history is based.

From personal experience I can assure you that in the Ph.D. programs at most universities, to question the assertions of the so-called leaders in the field is to find yourself denied access to the programs. Free thinkers are neither tolerated nor wanted, as they tend to ask questions that might upset the apple cart. However, if you are of liberal bent and blindly parrot the speculations of the instructors who generally made their own grades upon their demonstrated allegiance to their mentors' interpretation of history, you can do well.

As an example, in one Ph.D. level Middle Eastern history class this writer took at the University of Texas at El Paso (UTEP), the main focus of the class was on the wonders of Islam and the fact that homosexuality was misunderstood and an important aspect of this very advanced religion. To question these tenets got you out of the Ph.D. program quickly[1].

However, be that as it may, it was clear that the question of how these ancient civilizations achieved their levels of sophistication was not something that was to be discussed since the illuminating lights in the field of archeology had made their pronouncements eons ago (most in the late 1800's or early 1900's) and were not to be questioned today. However, it is the main thrust of this work that these leading lights, as it where, all started with the premise that the older a civilization, the more primitive it became and ignored any evidence to the contrary.

This work is not to denigrate the work of such giants in the field as Howard Carter, Lord Carnarvon and others, but rather to question some of their basic beliefs. Archaeology was originally not a field of scientific inquiry as the basic theories were created on the fly as it were as new discoveries were dug up from the Egyptian sands.

---

[1] It was also interesting to note that military veterans were kicked to the curb as fast as humanly possible since most Ph.D.'s teaching in this program were so left leaning as to make one question how they could actually walk upright.

The field of Archaeology actually got its start in the 19th century. Archaeology had its start in the European study of history and in people who were interested in the past (dare I say amateurs). King Nabonidus (556-539 BCE), the last king of the Neo-Babylonian Empire, was interested in the past so he could align himself with past glories. He led a revitalization movement and rebuilt ancient temples.

Early systemic investigation and Historiography can be traced back to the Greek historian Herodotus (c. 484-c. 425). He was the first western scholar to systematically collect artifacts and test their accuracy. He was also the first to make a compelling narrative of the past. He is known for his set of 9 books called **The Histories**, in which he wrote of everything he could find out about different regions. A few examples are he discussed the causes and consequences of the Greco-Persian Wars. He also explored the Nile and Delphi. However, scholars have found errors in his records and believe he probably did not go as far south down the Nile as he said he did.

As defined, archaeology is the study of human activity through the recovery and analysis of material culture. The archaeological record [2] consists

---

[2] The archaeological record is the body of physical (not written) evidence about the past. It is one of the core concepts in archaeology, the academic discipline concerned with documenting and interpreting the archaeological record. Archaeological theory is used to

of artifacts, architecture, biofacts or ecofacts, and cultural landscapes. Archaeology can be considered both a social science and a branch of the humanities. In North America, archaeology is considered a sub-field of anthropology, while in Europe archaeology is often viewed as either a discipline in its own right or a sub-field of other disciplines.

Archaeologists study human prehistory and history, from the development of the first stone tools at Lomekwi in East Africa 3.3 million years ago up until recent decades. Archaeology as a field is distinct from the discipline of paleontology, the study of fossil remains. Archaeology is particularly important for learning about prehistoric societies, for whom there may be no written records to study. Prehistory includes over 99% of the human past, from the Paleolithic until the advent of literacy in societies across the world. Archaeology has various goals, which range from understanding culture history to reconstructing past lifeways to

---

interpret the archaeological record for a better understanding of human cultures. The archaeological record can consist of the earliest ancient findings as well as contemporary artifacts. Human activity has had a large impact on the archaeological record. Destructive human processes, such as agriculture and land development, may damage or destroy potential archaeological sites. Other threats to the archaeological record include natural phenomena and scavenging. Archaeology can be a destructive science for the finite resources of the archaeological record are lost to excavation. Therefore archaeologists limit the amount of excavation that they do at each site and keep meticulous records of what is found. The archaeological record is the record of human history, of why civilizations prosper or fail and why cultures change and grow. It is the story of the world that humans have created.

documenting and explaining changes in human societies through time.

In spite of the popular belief that archeologists just dig "old stuff up", the field of archeology today, involves surveying, excavation and eventually analysis of data collected to learn more about the past. In broad scope, archaeology relies on cross-disciplinary research. It also draws upon the following fields:

- Anthropology,
- History,
- Art history,
- Classics,
- Ethnology,
- Geography,
- Geology,
- Literary history,
- Linguistics,
- Semiology,
- Textual criticism,
- Physics,
- Information sciences,
- Chemistry,
- Statistics,
- Paleoecology,

- Paleography,
- Paleontology,
- Paleozoology, and
- Paleobotany.

Modern archaeology developed out of antiquarianism in Europe during the 19th century, and has since become a discipline practiced across the world. Many rank amateurs who had money would spend their winters in Egypt conducting their idea of an archeological dig, which, in many cases, dissolved into a treasure hunt. Archaeology has been used by nation-states to create particular visions of the past. Since its early development, various specific sub-disciplines of archaeology have developed, including maritime archaeology, feminist archaeology and archaeo-astronomy, and numerous different scientific techniques have been developed to aid archaeological investigation.

Nonetheless, today, archaeologists face many problems, such as dealing with pseudo-archaeology[3] (a category into which many will toss this work), the looting of artifacts, a lack of public interest, and opposition to the excavation of human remains. However, in spite of these high sounding scientific methods brought to bear on the issue of the past, the fact still remains that

---

[3] New or original ideas are, normally, immediately labeled as pseudo-archaeology by the leaders in the field without impartial examination.

the parameters of these research projects are still controlled by ideas developed by "the leaders" in the field as will be shown.

Most archaeologists have their pet theories on how history progressed and when certain things happened. Those who are successful in the field normally had mentors who gave them a leg up so to speak and he mentors had their own pet theories. A Prime example is long running argument over the age of the Egyptian Sphinx.

The Sphinx water erosion hypothesis contends that the main type of weathering evident on the enclosure walls of the Great Sphinx was caused by prolonged and extensive rainfall that would have predated the time of Djedefre and Khafre, the Pharaohs credited by most modern Egyptologists with building the Great Sphinx and Second Pyramid at Giza around 2500 BC. Egyptologists, geologists and others have rejected the water erosion hypothesis and the idea of an older Sphinx, offering various alternative explanations for the cause and date of the erosion[4].

R. A. Schwaller de Lubicz [5], a French mystic and alternative Egyptologist, first claimed evidence of water erosion on

---

[4] In most cases they reject the water erosion theory because it was a climatologist who first gained prominence for this theory not an archaeologist. Additionally, the theory flies in the face of the time lines developed by early leaders in the field so it could not be correct.

[5] **René Adolphe Schwaller de Lubicz** (December 7, 1887 – 1961), born René Adolphe Schwaller in Alsace-Lorraine, was a French occultist, student

the walls of the Sphinx enclosure in the 1950s. John Anthony West, an author and alternative Egyptologist, investigated Schwaller de Lubicz's ideas further and, in 1989, sought the opinion of Robert M. Schoch, a geologist and associate professor of natural science at the College of General Studies at Boston University.

From his investigation of the enclosure's geology, Schoch concluded the main type of weathering evident on the Sphinx enclosure walls was caused by prolonged and extensive rainfall. According to Schoch, the area has experienced a mean annual rainfall of approximately one inch (2.5 cm) since the Old Kingdom (c. 2686 – 2134 BC), such that, since Egypt's last period of significant rainfall ended between the late fourth and early 3rd millennium BC, the Sphinx's construction must date to the 6th or 5th millennium BC.

Schoch further notes the same heavy precipitation-induced weathering as seen on the walls of the Sphinx enclosure is also found on the core blocks of the Sphinx and Valley Temples, both known to have been originally constructed from blocks taken from the Sphinx enclosure when the body was carved. Though the presence of extensive 4th Dynasty repair work to the Sphinx and

---

of sacred geometry and Egyptologist known for his twelve-year study of the art and architecture of the Temple of Luxor in Egypt and his subsequent book *The Temple In Man*.[1]

associated temples is acknowledged by such Egyptologists as Lehner and Hawass, Schoch contends: "*Therefore if the granite facing is covering deeply weathered limestone, the original limestone structures must predate by a considerable degree the granite facing. Obviously, if the limestone cores (originating from the Sphinx ditch) of the temples predate the granite ashlars (granite facings), and the granite ashlars are attributable to Khafre of the Fourth Dynasty, then the Great Sphinx was built prior to the reign of Khafre.*"

Colin Reader, a British geologist, agrees that the suggested evidence of weathering indicates prolonged water erosion. Reader found, inter alia, that the flow of rainwater causing the weathering had been stemmed by the construction of 'Khufu's quarries', which lie directly "upstream" of the Sphinx enclosure, and therefore concludes that the Sphinx must predate the reign of Khufu (2589 – 2566 BC), and certainly Khafre, by several hundred years. Reader disagrees with Schoch's palaeo-meteorological estimates, and instead concludes that the Sphinx dates to the Early Dynastic Period (c. 3150 – 2686 BC). To explain the disproportionate size of the head compared to the body, Reader, as does Schoch, also suggests the head of the Sphinx was originally that of a lion and recarved sometime later in the likeness of a pharaoh[6].

---

[6] Rank speculation is permissible by archaeologists to protect a cherished theory, however, indulging in speculation is not allowed by those who

Similarly, David Coxill, a geologist working independently of both Schoch and Reader, has concluded from the evidence of weathering in the enclosure that *"[t]he Sphinx is at least 5,000 years old and pre-dates dynastic times [before 3100 BC]."*

Zahi Hawass, former Egyptian minister of state for antiquities affairs and secretary-general of the Supreme Council of Antiquities, was asked in an interview on the PBS series NOVA if it was possible that a more ancient civilization might have sculpted the Sphinx. Hawass replied: *"Of course it is not possible for one reason .... No single artifact, no single inscription, or pottery, or anything has been found until now, in any place to predate the Egyptian civilization more than 5,000 years ago[7]."*

This reasoning and conclusion was supported in a similar NOVA interview of Mark Lehner, another senior Egyptologist. Other archaeologists who have made similar criticisms include Kenneth Feder[8].

---

question an accepted theory. Also note that those who question the age of the Sphinx are not archaeologist but from other fields of science. For an archaeologist to question such a thing would not be politically correct and would end their flow of grant dollars to carry out their work.

[7] We will be talking about a number of items that pre-date 5,000 years ago in this text. Also, it should be remembered that the basement of almost every museum in the world is full of artifacts that do not fit into the accepted timeframe of accepted history as defined by archaeologists. You will see numerous examples of artifacts that are out of context as we move through this work. Make up your own minds.

[8] **Kenneth L. "Kenny" Feder** (born August 1, 1952) is a professor of archaeology at Central Connecticut State University and the author of several books on archaeology and criticism of pseudo-archaeology such

A different argument used by Egyptologists to ascribe the Sphinx to Khafra is the "context" theory, which notes that the Sphinx is located in the context of the funerary complex surrounding the Second Pyramid, which is traditionally[9] connected with Khafra. Apart from the Causeway, the Pyramid and the Sphinx, the complex also includes the Sphinx Temple and the Valley Temple, both of which display the same architectural style, with 100-tonne stone blocks quarried out of the Sphinx enclosure.

A diorite statue of Khafre, which was discovered buried upside down along with other debris in the Valley Temple, is claimed as support for the Khafra theory. Reader agrees that the Sphinx Temple and Valley Temple are closely associated with the Sphinx, as is the Causeway and even part of the Khafra Mortuary Temple, but suggests this evidence merely indicates these structures also predate Khafra and does not link the Sphinx in any way to Khafra.

Rainer Stadelmann, former director of the German Archaeological Institute in Cairo suggests Khufu, Khafre's father, was the builder of the Sphinx and contends Khafra's Causeway

---

as *Frauds, Myths, and Mysteries: Science and Pseudoscience in Archaeology.* His book Encyclopedia *of* Dubious *Archaeology: From Atlantis to the Walam Olum* was published in 2010. His newest book "Ancient America: Fifty Archaeological Sites to See for Yourself" was published in 2017. He is the founder and director of the Farmington River Archaeological Project.

[9] In other words, it is not accepted to question tradition if you are an archaeologist.

was built to conform to a pre-existing structure which he concludes, given its location, could only have been the Sphinx. Lehner's official website also offers a similar argument based on an Archaeological sequence of structures built in the area. Lehner points to the way several structures in the area incorporate elements from older structures, and based on the order in which they were constructed concludes that the archaeological sequencing does not allow for a date older than the reign of Khafra.

Hawass points to the poor quality of much of the Giza limestone as the basis for the significant erosion levels. He has concluded, from the present-day rapid rate of erosion on the Member II surface of the Sphinx, that *"[t]he eleven hundred years between Khafre and the first major restoration in the Eighteenth Dynasty, or even half this time, would have been more than enough to erode the Member II into the deep recesses behind Phase I restoration masonry"*.

Schoch states that other structures and surfaces on the Giza Plateau are made from the same band of limestone as the Sphinx enclosure, but they do not show the same erosion as the walls of the Sphinx enclosure.

Peter Lacovara, an Egyptologist and curator at the M. C. Carlos Museum in Emory University, assigns "some of the erosional features" on the enclosure walls to quarrying activities rather than weathering, and states that other wear and tear on the Sphinx itself is due to groundwater percolation and wind erosion.

So you have Ph.D.'s in archaeology defending their traditional beliefs against new ideas brought by Ph.D.'s in other fields of study. They defend these beliefs with almost a religious fervor as result of having built their career around them. Most of the leaders in the field have written extensively (remember in academia it is publish or perish and heaven help you if you are found to be wrong in what you publish) about their beliefs and are loath to have to admit that they could perhaps be wrong.

So with this groundwork set, let us continue in our journey through the world of Ancient Secrets. If the reader keeps an open mind, he or she might just be surprised to find that our civilization is not the epitome of advancement that it is touted to be.

CHAPTER TWO

COULD THE BIBLE BE CORRECT?

Today it is fashionable in academia to pooh-pooh many of the statements found in the Bible. This writer has heard the Bible referred to by university professors as the best selling fairy tale in the world. Certainly, a critical review will show that the Bible is filled with errors and mistakes. After all, what we know as the Holy Bible was written eons ago and then modified as political and religious thought changed over the years. More accurately, it was based on much earlier works from earlier civilizations.

As an example of how man has changed what it believed by millions to be the unadulterated Word of God, in 325 AD, Roman Emperor Caesar Flavius Constantine I called the First Ecumenical Council of the Christian Church to meet in the city of Nicea[10]. The purpose of this unprecedented meeting of church bishops and other church leaders was to define the nature of God for all of Christianity and eliminate confusion, controversy and contention within the church. In other words, this meeting of

---

[10] Nicea was located in Asia Minor, east of Constantinople.

important and influential religious leaders was to set out, for all time and all peoples under the Empire what they were to believe in so far as their God was concerned.

What became known as Christianity was not based on some thunderous event with basic truths handed down from the mountain top or the teachings of a wandering carpenter, but rather what we have come to know as Christianity was established during a business meeting specifically called to determine what people would be told from the pulpit by the religious leaders of the day.

It was the Council of Nicea that determined by a majority vote of those attending on that particular day that Jesus Christ was an eternal deity, that he was the physical Son of God and defined the relationship between the Father and the Son as one of substance. This meeting also affirmed that the Trinity, the Father, the Son and the Holy Spirit were to be listed and taught that they were deemed to be three co-equal and co-eternal Persons.

Since in the experience of this writer if you have three religious leaders in the same room you have four opinions espoused it is therefore unusual to see such agreement. However, under the threat of punishment by the Emperor, this group of over 300 very human religious leaders made the major decisions as to how God and Jesus would be worshipped in the Roman Empire. Just as IBM tells its managers what to say to maintain the corporate image, so these 300 Christian leaders were told what to say and what not to say to maintain their corporate, religious image and keep their cushy jobs. The Emperor wanted no rebels in the ranks of the Bishops.

The ultimate organization of what became known to history, as the Roman Catholic Church was not some inspired vision of a religious fanatic who walked the sands of ancient Palestine. Nor was it a popular movement that changed the face of religion, but it was rather a business decision of a Roman Emperor who wanted tighter control of his subjects and the orders were given to the Council at Nicea that uniformity of message was needed in order to strengthen their control over the masses who reverently believed what their religious leaders told them.

However, it must be kept in mind that these issues were decided by a majority vote of very human people, not religious saints, whose very livelihood depended on the belief and devotion of the lower classes in the message that they were teaching was the true word of God. The decisions at Nicea were purely business decisions, not religious ones.

Roman Emperor Constantine, who claimed to have converted to Christianity as a result of a vision just before a major battle, had called for this meeting of bishops to be held in Nicea to resolve some serious controversies among church leaders. These doctrinal issues were threatening to tear the Christian Church and ultimately the Roman Empire apart. By the time Constantine had taken ultimate control of the Empire, the Roman Empire was failing, there was dissension in the nobility and there had already been several civil wars or insurrections.

The Empire had already been divided into the Western Empire and the Eastern Empire and even with these changes there were obvious problems. The citizens of the Roman Empire worshiped a variety of gods under a variety of names. Christianity was just one of a large number of religions to be found within the Empire. The Emperor saw a cohesive religion such as Christianity as a tool he could use to strengthen the empire during this period of trouble and was determined to force the 300 or so church leaders to get behind one doctrine.

It was not some inspired Church leader or some mandate form the mount that confirmed Jesus's divinity. It seemed to have been the apostles who knew and followed Jesus Christ that decided that Jesus was the physical Son of God and number two in the Trinity so this belief of twelve disparate followers of this little known religious leader was what the Bishops decided to make canonical law. This belief would be doctrine and it was affirmed by a majority vote, though it was a close vote with a large number of bishops espousing the belief that Jesus was a physical being who lived and died, perhaps a major prophet to be sure, but a physical being none-the-less.

The religious tenet that he was an eternal being was not some dictate from God or a well documented fact but rather a purely business decision to solidify the Church behind what was already written in the scriptures [11] which had come from the Apostles. For anyone to teach anything else would be considered heresy and bring punishment.

In order to solidify control over the early Church and the masses that so fanatically believed what they heard from their religious leaders, there was a necessity that the religious message must be controlled by the powers that be. To do this, the early Church had to also control the history of the Church, which meant that what was contained in the religious writings of the day also had to be controlled. This also included the letters written by the Apostles to various churches.

---

[11] It was the Apostles who elevated Jesus from being a man to being the physical son of God which is very much like the inner circle of every would be messiah proclaiming that their candidate was the true anointed of God and should be worshipped. How is this different from someone such as David Koresh? It must also be realized that the Church was, first an foremost a business, one that the Emperor recognized could be a major cash cow for the Roman Empire. It is also a very strong control element. God never issued a proclamation that each person should tithe 10% of their income to the Church; it was the leaders of the Church who made this decision and said that this is what God desired. After all, how else would they get paid and have a roof over their heads unless the faithful paid for it. How is this different from the U.S. Government deciding that each person must pay taxes to pay for government workers salaries and government services?

In final analysis, no one really decided what went into the work called the Holy Bible. These same religious scholars at the Council of Nicea developed a definition as to what qualified as a Scripture and the various religious books had to meet this definition. This definition included five characteristics, called the Law of Canonicity.

The Jewish Scripture from Palestine is what is referred to as the Old Testament. This is what Jesus referred to in the Book of Luke, Chapter 24, Verse 44 when he spoke of the Law of Moses. Outside what is referred to as the Holy Land there were 12 to 15 other religious books that were also looked at by many as being part of the Scripture.

The Septaugint, which was translated in Egypt contained books that are now referred to as Apocrypha. Some early sects of Christianity included the Apocrypha as part of the Scripture and other sects did not, which led to differences in religious belief. As a result of these differences, the Emperor ordered that the written message [12] as well as the verbal teachings needed to be standardized.

It is said that at the First Council of Nicea, the Council of Bishops was given to task of determining what writings were to

---

[12] It should be remembered that the vast majority of the people at this time could not read. However, the Church believed that to not standardize the written message could lead to later confusion and possible a loss of power and control.

considered by the Church as divinely inspired and which should be destroyed [13] so as to not contaminate the minds of the masses. Some have complained that many things in the Bible seem to contradict other things written and that the books contained within the Bible are not in any type of chronological order. It should be remembered that the compilation of the Bible was a very complicated undertaking involving church leaders of many different beliefs, in an atmosphere of dissension, jealousy, intolerance, persecution and bigotry.

It should also be remembered that at this time Christianity was merely a rather unimportant sect in the Roman Empire, not a major religion. Christianity received its designation as a major religion as a result of Emperor Constantine's decision to make it the official religion of the Roman Empire. Therefore, the question of the divinity of Jesus was one that threatened to destroy the relatively new religion [14] before it really got started. The bottom line of their marching orders from Emperor Constantine was that he did not care what the Council of Bishops ultimately believed or taught as long as they were united in their teachings and they supported his authority as Emperor.

---

[13] All copies that could be found of those religious books not approved by the early church were normally collected up and burned.

[14] It should also be remembered that just as the Roman Senate could make the Emperor a God by majority vote, so too could the Christian Church made Jesus a god (or at least divine) by a majority vote.

The Church was at a crossroads in history; this little known religious sect was offered the position of the official religion for the most powerful country in the known world in return for their support of his reign. Constantine also believed that by compiling a book of what were called sacred writings, this book would give authority to the new church and the new church would support his own authority.

This mandate also put these 300 or so Bishops in a position to create what was essentially a new religion. The most influential of the Bishops would naturally have the highest positions and reap the majority of the benefits. Thus there was a great deal of backroom dealing in determining exactly what this new religion would believe or not believe.

Make no mistake, at this point, the teachings of Jesus and the early Church and even of the Apostles mattered little in the final analysis. It was what could be used to increase the power of the Church and be sold to the Emperor and ultimately the uneducated masses that made up the Roman Empire as the word of God that was the most important aspect of the Council of Nicea.

Frankly, we do not really know what was taught by the Bishops, as scripture, prior to the Council of Nicea. There were many books written by supposed prophets in circulation that took opposing positions in regard to religious issues. Many of those at the Council referred to as Bishops taught different things about

Jesus and God. Therefore, it was a major issue for the Council to determine which of the teachings and beliefs would be given Imperial approval [15] and, which would be destroyed. In the fanaticism of the era if a book was not approved as a true Scripture, all copies of these books were usually ordered burned, by Imperial Decree, as the work of the Devil. To not obey this decree was to suffer an automatic death sentence.

It is also said that Jesus spoke of reincarnation, but these teachings were removed from the teachings of the Church and ultimately the Scripture. This was not just a cosmetic change, but also an issue that many Bishops felt was very important to solidifying their power. After all, if a soul lived numerous times, it was believed that they could ignore the Church teachings and still ultimately go the Heaven by following the teachings in a later life. So the issue was that by teaching that a soul only lived once, it was felt that this would make believers toe the line when it came to religious teachings and the mandates of the Church[16].

---

[15] There was a story that Constantine was unsure what books should be included in the final edition of what would become the Scripture, so he was said to have taken all of the books given to him to review, threw them onto a table. The ones that stayed on the table remained in the final Scripture and those that fell off of the table were ordered removed from consideration. I guess this was similar to the unofficial motto of the Airborne, kill them all and let God sort them out. This is, it is God's will as to which books stayed on the table. Could work, I guess.

[16] You might wonder how even the power of the Emperor could get over 300 religious leaders to agree on something so important as the creation of the "message." There is a story that the final vote as to the adhesion to what

THE AFTERMATH OF THE COUNCIL OF NICEA

Make no mistake Emperor Constantine was very serious about the end result of the Council of Nicea. He used the power of the Empire to enforce the decisions of "his" religion and the power of the Church to ensure that the citizens of the Empire were taught to respect his power.

Socrates makes mention in Book 1, Chapter 8 of Historia Ecclesia that Constantine exiled Bishop Arius and some of his supporters for refusing to submit to the decisions of the Council. It also quotes a letter by Constantine ordering the destruction of all works composed by Arius on pain of death to any found holding any of these banned works and refers to an earlier letter regarding the works of Bishop Porphyry.

In Book 1, Chapter 21 of Historia Ecclesia, Sozomen writes that Emperor Constantine wrote to all the cities of the Empire ordering the destruction of the works of Bishop Arius and his followers, and instituted the death penalty for those who refused the Imperial order to destroy them. So clearly, the newly re-organized Christian religion was not just for those whose belief system leaned that way, but rather an Imperial Edict that would be

---

was called the creed showed that all but five supported the final version. Negotiation and "arm twisting" reduced this number to two, but the final two would not budge. So, to solve the issue, the two, Theonas of Marmarica and Secundus of Ptolemaid, were exiled and anathematized. Another Bishop by the name of Arius was also anathematized and his writings were all destroyed by being burned. A good way to end and argument – exile your foes.

obeyed. If the masses worshiped any god, it would be the God of the Christian faith.

By the same token, other ancient texts also have errors and mistakes, but this isn't a problem because people don't expect the authors of those texts to be perfect. The Bible, in contrast, is claimed by many believers, to include the Bishops of the Council of Nicea and the Emperor Constantine, to be infallible, inerrant and perfect. Each of the authors represented in the approved Bible have long been said to be inspired by God as they wrote.

Many millions of Christians base their entire religious ideology around the presumption that the Bible is free from errors or mistakes, so to opponents of Christianity demonstrating the presence of errors is one of the major keys to rebutting their religious claims.

Scientific errors — statements that conflict with facts about reality we have learned through scientific investigation — can be found throughout the Bible because the biblical texts were written at times when human knowledge about our world was quite limited. We can't blame ancient writers for knowing less than we do now, but we can blame people alive now for preferring the errors of ancient writers over the reliable knowledge developed today. At the same time there are some purported scientific errors that may actually be based on undiscovered truths.

As an example, much is made in the Bible about individuals such as Methuselah living over 900 years. This is clearly wrong as we all know, since the average human life span is the fabled 3 score and 10, correct? Well, this may not be an error after all.

Well, the next question is sure to be how can this be possible? Surely, no human can live almost a thousand years. However, it has now been discovered, or perhaps rediscovered that there is a way to artificially extend human life far beyond the normal. This is through the use of monatomic gold is said by some to be a gift of the Annunaki, the sky gods. Only those smiled upon by the Annunaki would be offered the gift of eternal life.

Writers and researchers such as Zecharia Sitchin[17] have written much on these early times and the beliefs of what many believe to be the oldest civilization on the planet, that of Summer.

---

[17] Sitchin, Zacharia, the 12th Planet, Harper Nonfiction, New York, (1998)

CHAPTER THREE

A GIFT OF THE GODS

In the 1970's, David Hudson, a so-called Republican and cotton farmer from Phoenix, Arizona made a most interesting discovery. This discovery involved the manipulation of energy at the atomic-level and according to many his discovery (or rediscovery) may have opened the door to limitless free energy, cures for AIDS and cancer, longevity, faster than light speed, anti-gravity and much more in the way of very advanced marvels[18].

Mr. Hudson began speaking publicly about his research and discoveries in 1995, when at that time he pointed out the multiple connections between the works of Zecharia Sitchin[19], the Annunaki, the Tree of Life, The Egyptian Book of the Dead, Alchemy, Immanuel Velikovsky, Superconductivity, Ark of the Covenant, The Adam's Family, and more recently the works of

---

[18] Marrs, Jim, The Illuminati: The Secret Society that Hijacked the World, Visible Ink Press, Detroit. MI 2017.
[19] Sitchin, Zecharia, The 12th Planet, 1976, The Stairway to Heaven, 1980, The Wars of Gods and Men, 1985, The Lost Realms, When Time Began, Genesis Revisited, 1990, Divine Encounters, 1995, Avon Books, New York.

Laurence Gardner [20]. There are also numerous researchers interested in a variation on the ORME, the ORMUS, where it is assumed that the working material is not necessary mono-atomic, but may be diatomic — consisting of two (or more) atoms of the precious metals[21].

This very strange material, which we will refer to as white powder gold, had a number of very unusual properties. In the rest of this chapter, we are reproducing the contents published on line as an overview of Mr. Hudson's discovery. It is well worth reading.

The story of Mr. Hudson's efforts over the years is given in the form of a rough transcript of his presentation in 1995 at the International Forum on New Science in Fort Collins, Colorado. As such, it serves as an excellent introduction to the study of the ORME, and its immense implications. His story and the profound revelations of his work are well worth considerable study. This is only the beginning introduction.

---

[20] Gardner, Laurence, Bloodline of the Holy Grail (1996) and (1997), Barnes and Noble Books, New York; Genesis of the Grail Kings, 1999, Bantam Press, New York; Realm of the Ring Lords, 2000, Media Quest, Ottery St. Mary, England; and most importantly: Lost Secrets of the Sacred Ark, Amazing Revelations of the Incredible Powers of Gold, 2003, Harper Collins.

[21] This material comes from the following website that discusses Mr. Hudson: https://monatomic-orme.com

DAVID HUDSON AT IFNS

I was buying gold and silver as an inflation hedge. Then got into producing gold from a natural source, old mining sources. Mining worked well with the farming. You beat Uncle Sam as much as possible out of taxes, and at the same time accumulate as much wealth as you can. Leaching gold with cyanide process is like leaching salt out in the farming process. More of a hobby than a business — no intention of making money. But something I enjoyed very much. Did it for fun.

In the process of recovering gold and silver, I began to recover something else, which was causing losses of the gold and silver. Eventually, it reached the point where the gold and silver would not recover at all because of the something else. I then shut it down, to find out what the problem material was. I am not a physicist or a chemist and had no idea what the stuff was. It would recover and had a specific gravity; it would recover in the molten lead like it was gold and silver; it would flow out of the lead; but when I held the lead down, I had nothing. The mining community refers to this as "ghost gold", a non-assayable, non-identifiable form of gold.

I then became involved with someone who does emission spectroscopy (ES) and became aware of work done by the Soviet Academy of Sciences. When one does ES, it involves taking a carbon electrode, placing your sample on the carbon electrode, and then running a second carbon electrode down above it, and striking an arc. When you strike the arc, the elements ionize and give off specific light frequencies. This is spectroscopic analysis. In the analysis, it's done for 10-15 seconds before the electrode is burned away, and American Spectroscopists claim that anything there will be ionized and read within those 15 minutes.

My sample was identified as Iron, Silicon, and Aluminum. I then spent three years in finding ways to take away all the Fe, Si, and Al. Then, I still had 98% of the sample of the material. On the arc, the material didn't indicate to be anything. It was nothing. Back to Cornell University, where I worked with a Ph.D., who did X-Ray Analysis. This involved: Cumming Microscopy, Diffraction Microscopy, Fluorescent Microscopy, and five other wonderful technologies. The Ph.D. said that it was Iron, Silicon, and Aluminum. Stayed there to remove it all.

After that, the Ph.D. said it was "pure nothing." This wasn't good enough for me. I could hold it in my hands, weigh it, perform chemistries with it — it was something. I then recalled that, according to the Soviet Academy of Sciences, the proper analytical tool is to burn the sample in the emission spectroscopic analysis for 300 seconds, not just 15.

To do this, you have to sheath the electrode with an inert gas — keeping all the oxygen away from the DC arc. Otherwise, the carbon oxidizes, and the electrode falls apart. I set up to do this, using Argon gas to sheath the electrode — keeping the oxygen away. Because carbon is a very high-temperature material, it will then last for 300 seconds. When the material was placed on the electrode and the arc was struck, there was no reading at all for 15 seconds [other than "electronic grass" on the scope, as well as Iron, Silicon, Aluminum, and occasionally, traces of Calcium]. Then the material went quiet.

[Argon gas if fundamentally crucial to Sonoluminescence, as well. It also has an identical crystalline structure to such elements as Rhodium and Iridium.]

Figure 1: David Hudson

Finally, after 90 seconds, Palladium (Pd) began to read; after 110 seconds, Platinum (Pt) began to read; at 130 seconds,

Ruthenium (Ru); at about 140-150 seconds, Rhodium; at 190 seconds, Iridium; at 220 seconds, Osmium began to read. The Russians call this fractional vaporization. For example, when one has water in an iron container, you can't get the iron hotter than the boiling point of water as long as there is water present. This is the basis for cooling systems in engines, and why automobile engines don't overheat, as long as there is water present. But once the water is gone, the temperature rises very rapidly to the melting temperature of the iron.

[The temperature of any well-mixed solution undergoing a phase change will stay at the temperature of the phase change until the phase is completed. Also, the relevant boiling temperatures for the metals in the sample are: Calcium: 1420 oC, Iron: 1535 oC, Silicon: 2355 oC, Aluminum: 2327 oC; followed by: Palladium: >2200 oC, Rhodium: 2500 oC, Ruthenium: 4150 oC, Platinum: 4300 oC, Iridium: >4800 oC, Osmium: >5300 oC. (Silver has a boiling point of 1950 oC, while Gold's boiling point is 2600 oC.)]

Essentially, all of the emissions from the elements were coming off in the sequence of their increasing boiling temperatures. The maximum temperature of the DC arc is, theoretically, in the center of the arc, 5450 to 5500 oC; while the sample was slightly away from the center. Thus, all the heat went into boiling off one element at a time, in the sequence of their boiling temperatures. They come off individually as if there is nothing else in the sample.

I continued to run the sample for 2 and a half years, comparing it to standard samples. The amazing thing is that commercially available samples of the precious metals, when placed in the emission spectroscopic DC arc, read within 15 seconds. (And they assume they're reading it all.)

But then it goes quiet, until after 90 seconds, it starts to read again. About 85% of the reading occurs at the end. In effect, the people buying the commercially available samples and doing readings are only doing about 15 to 20% of the sample. And they assume it's everything. Short burn times don't do the trick. They assume the standard, and yet this is not the correct standard.

Keep in mind that the Soviet Academy of Sciences, the most prestigious scientific body in the Soviet Union and Johnson-Mathewe-Inglehart produce all the precious metals in the world. The mining activity of the best deposit in the world in South Africa for six of these elements (Pd, Pt, Os, Ru, Ir, and Rh — i.e. no silver or gold) may yield only one-third of one ounce of the precious metals per ton of ore. They go a half-mile down into the ground, following an 18-inch seam of material, to get 1/3 of 1 oz per ton of all the precious elements. No one else knows it's there, and no one can analyze it. We, on the other hand, can derive and identify out of one ton of ore: 6-8 ounces of Palladium, 12-13 ounces of Platinum, 150 ounces of Osmium, 250 ounces of Ruthenium, 600 ounces of Iridium, and 1200 ounces of Rhodium!!

This was then confirmed by a highly respected chemist and spectroscopy, including all of the colors of the solutions being correct, all the oxidation potentials were correct, all of the physical properties were correct. An analytical chemist. Consider Rhodium. Rhodium produces a crimson, blood red colored salt. That is how it got its name, from the rose-colored salt, and the only element which produces this color. Very conspicuous.

When you precipitate Rhodium out of solution, you add bromide as the oxidizer, and then you do a neutralization of the acid, and the hydroxide precipitates out of the solution. You filter it, dry it, oxidize it, hydrogen reduce it, and you should have metal. (Standard procedure). But we neutralized the solution of the pure Rhodium, got a red brown dioxide, filtered that out, dried it, and heated it in a tube furnace under oxygen up to 850 degrees for an hour to dehydrate it, and we'd get this red brown dioxide. Then we put it back in the tube furnace and hydrogen reduce it to a gray powder, and then take the gray powder in a tube furnace at 1000 degrees under argon, and it turned snow white.

A commercial spectroscopic firm then analyzed three samples, and again picked up Iron, Aluminum, Silicon, and Calcium. There was no consistency between the three samples, which were all the same. The material was 99.9% pure Rhodium, in different stages of the processing.

The standards that are sold as labeled as RhCl3, when in reality they are Rh12Cl36. It still has metal-metal bonds. Even without the Chlorine, you still have the metal bonds, which are never lost. But if you take Rhodium to the monatomic state, you can end up with HRhCl4. Then when you take away the Chloride, you get HRh (Hydrogen Rhodide). A Rhodide is a -1, instead of a +1. The physical properties are more like an Iodide.

When gold is produced as a monatomic gold, it's a forest green color. As a metal, it's a yellow gold. No one has monatomic gold as a commercial product. Monatomic gold is much more powerful, as in a fuel cell. Boiling gold will never result in a monatomic gold. Gold has the 5d, 6s1 electron structure (the single s electron, like Sodium, Potassium, Hydrogen, and Lithium), and is thus explosively reactive. Except that in the case of gold, it's gold reacting with gold.

But in the bowels of the earth, in the volcanoes, nature is producing monatomic gold. When it comes out, 98% of the gold coming out is monoatomic, 2% is metal. [Thus, Hudson may not be making monatomic gold, he is separating it instead.] We have worked with the yellow gold, converting it, but always coming back to yellow gold. But when we get monatomic gold, it never goes back to yellow. And as monatomic gold, it is not metallic, has none of the metallic qualities of yellow gold.

If you use thermo-gravimetric analysis, and you produce

monatomic gold, you get sort of a gray-black, Hydrogen Auride (HAu). When you heat it, and the proton is annealed away, this is the same way you produce Amorphous Silicon (Silane to Amorphous Silicon). When you heat it, the proton is annealed away; it goes to a snow-white powder! It loses 4/9th of its weight. If you take it back to metal, it regains the weight. As you kept annealing the material, it would levitate – taking the pan with it. In cooling, it would sometimes go to 2 or 300% of the weight. In heating, it goes to less than nothing.

This only happens in the white powder form. But mass has never left. Losing weight when cooling the material (approaching absolute zero), and you have a superconductor.

A superconductor is a material that has a single wavelength in the sample, a single vibration or frequency, much like a laser. By definition, a superconductor does not allow any voltage potential to exist within it; it's perfect amperage, but no voltage. To hook up wires with ordinary current to the superconductor and get the electrons off the wire, you need voltage. You have the tune the vibrational frequency of the electrons in the wire to that of the superconductors. And to get them off.

The electrons going into the superconductor have to pair, with a time forward electron with a time reverse electron. When they pair, they become light. Any amount of light can exist in the superconductor. It doesn't reside in any space-time. The only way to prove it's a superconductor is to measure a Meissner field. Non-polar field (only field of its kind). Superconductivity responds to magnetic fields. Earth's magnetic field is larger.

A superconductor can see your thoughts in your brain. Different parts of your brain light up when you eat something sweet or something sour — it's a superconductor that sees it.

When it goes to the white powder and loses 4/9th of its weight, it's flowing light within it, in response to the earth's magnetic field. And it flows so much current that it levitates 4/9th of its weight on the earth's magnetic field. A human hand has sufficient amperage, that if you pass it under the sample, the material floats. It's that sensitive to magnetic fields. All the eight precious metal elements can do this. Also Copper, Cobalt, and Nickel. So, I filed 11 patents. In 1990, my uncle showed me the Time-Life Book, *Secrets of the Alchemist*. I was not interested in Alchemy; I wanted credibility in physics and chemistry. The book talks about a "white powder of gold". The goal of the alchemist had been to make a "white powder of gold". To make "the container of the light of life." If you stand in its presence, you don't age. If you partake of it, you live forever. I begrudgingly agreed to read the book

I have since read some 500 books on alchemy, alchemy history, and it all goes back to a man named Enoch. Thoth, Hermes, Trigeminus. Same man. Ascended by partaking of the *white drops. He never died, instead ascended because he was so perfect.*

I found a huge amount of research going on in treating cancer with precious elements. That the elements have been found interacting with a cell by a vibrational frequency or by a light transfer and have been correcting the DNA. Any alteration, any defect in the DNA is corrected by the precious elements. It perfects the cells of our bodies. But the element going into our bodies is not a metal, the element is not a heavy metal, it is an element. So there's no heavy metal poisoning. You can eat any amount of this white flour, and it doesn't hurt you. If you eat it, it just goes through your digestive system.

I took some brain tissue from a pig, and some from a cow, and analyzed it. They destroyed the organic and did a metals analysis. Over 5% of the brain tissue by dry matter weight was Rhodium and Iridium. But no one knows it because it can't be directly measured. The elements are flowing the light of life in your body. The elements are in fact what the light is. There are four papers by the U.S. Naval Research that they have proved the cells communicate with each other by a process identical to superconductivity. But they can't figure out the physical mechanism.

It is the stealth atoms. It's the atoms in our bodies. However, no one knows they're there because they don't identify them by instrumental analysis. And the reason they don't identify them is also in the literature. Since 1986, the top physicists in the world, at the Niels Bohr Institute, at Argonne National Laboratory, at Brookhaven... They have found that there is a group of elements in the center of the Periodic Table that go through this strange state of existence.

So most of these publications occurred between 1988 on, but my patents were filed first. What they have found is that the nucleus of these elements were deformed, went to a high spin state — what's called high spin nuclei — and theoretically, these high spin nuclei should be superconductors because high spin nuclei pass energy from one atom to the next with no loss of energy.

This is what is in our bodies. This is what flows the light of life. And when you understand that a superconductor flows a single wavelength of light, but, in fact, the light is a null light, two ways that are mirror images of each other. There's no wave — it appears to cancel, but the null wave is in fact, while not measurable directly, is what produces the aura around our bodies. The aura is the Meissner field of superconductivity.

In our bodies, we have all this junk DNA. There are 30 aspects of the DNA that nobody can figure out what it's there for. We only use 15% of our brain. What's the other 85% of it there for? Did we evolve a brain we don't use? It's as if we had, at one time, a higher state of enlightenment, and we have fallen into the state we exist in now.

In ancient Egypt, which I traced this back to, there's a book, called *The Egyptian Book of the Dead and the Papyrus of Ani,* by Budge. This is the oldest book of the dead, from Old Kingdom Egypt. They found it, dating from about 3500 B.C.E., in the tomb of Pepi II. It says, "I am purified of all imperfections. What is it? I ascend like the golden hawk of Horus. What is it? I pass by the immortals without dying. What is it? I come before my father in Heaven. What is it?"

It goes on and on and on. It keeps asking this question, "What is it?"

The Hebrews worked in Egypt for many, many generations — they were the artisans and the metallurgists. When they left Egypt, Baalzelael, the goldsmith and Moses prepared the bread of the presence of God. He prepared the bread that the high priest partook of, the Melchizedek priest. The word in Hebrew that means, "What is it?" is manna. The word, manna, literally translates, verbatim, into a question, "What is it?" If you don't believe it, look in the Travels of Josephus. The very same words that were used in Old Kingdom Egypt, 3500 B.C. [Pepi II reigned 90 years from c. 2300 to 2210 (traditional dating), or 1720 to 1630 (Immanuel Velikovsky's dating).]

These elements are naturally in your body. It's primarily Rhodium and Iridium. Now the Bible says that Moses told the

Hebrew people, "You have not kept the covenant, and so the manna is being taken from you. But it will come back in the end times. When we will be a nation of high priests, not an elect high priesthood." This is the food, the light, you take in your body.

If you ask a Rabbi, have you ever heard of the white powder of gold, he'll say yes, we've heard of it, but to our knowledge, no one has known how to make it since the destruction of the First Temple. The Temple of Solomon. This knowledge has been lost. But it wasn't completely lost, the high priests when they left the temple when it was destroyed, went out on the desert and organized a commune called Qumran. They were the Essenes. In The Dead Seas Scrolls Uncovered [Eisement and Wise] this in ancient times, when the white powder was mixed in water, was known as The Golden Tear from the Eye of Horus. It was called, "That which issues from the mouth of the creator." The spittle. Not the word of God, but the spittle. Or the semen of the father in heaven. If you put the white powder in water, it doesn't dissolve. It forms this gelatinous suspension and looks just like a vial of semen. Being a farmer, I know what semen looks like.

The symbolism of "prepare yourself like a bride in the bridal chamber", purify and cleanse yourself, prepare yourself for the coming of the Father in heaven, to be inseminated by the father in heaven in the bridal chamber. To totally be regenerated, to be purified, to be cleansed. Every cell in your body will be taken back to the way it's supposed to be, when you were a teenager or a child. It perfects the DNA. And it flows the light until you reach the point where the light body exceeds the physical body.

In ancient Egypt, they said you have a physical body you must feed to grow as it's meant to be. If you don't feed that child, he'll never grow. He'll never become the person he's supposed to be. But you also have to feed the spirit body, you have to feed the ka, what they called it in ancient Egypt — so it can grow and become what it's meant to be. And most of you aren't feeding your ka. It's sitting there like a little runt inside your body. And they said you feed it and feed it and feed it with the semen of the father in heaven, and it grows and grows and becomes more enlightened and more enlightened, and you reach the point where the light body exceeds the physical body. You light up the room when you walk in.

The gifts that go with this are: perfect telepathy, you can know good and evil when it's in the room with you, you also can project your thoughts into someone else's mind. You can levitate; you can walk on water because it's flowing so much light within you that you don't attract gravity. And when you understand that when you exclude all external magnetic fields, when you exclude gravity, you are no longer of this space-time. You become a fifth-dimensional being. You can think where you would like to be, and go there. Just disappear. You also have other attributes that they go into. You can heal by the laying on of hands, and can cleanse and resurrect the dead within two or three days after they died. You have so much energy that you can embrace people and bring light and energy back into them.

Sounds pretty far out. Most groups don't receive this very well.

If this is really what this stuff does, then let's use it. I haven't achieved everything yet, but it miraculously has cured every disease that we've tested on thus far. Started with very incremental amounts of 2 mg (32,000 mg in an ounce), and have gone up to 50 mg — 50 mg over a period of 60 to 90 days, cures cancer, AIDS. It's the light that corrects itself. You all know this.

Christ said to his disciples, "Don't touch me, I don't have on my earthly garments." They asked, "When will we see you again?" He replied, "When you have prepared the proper food and have on your proper garments." What is the proper food? It's the food of the angels, the food of the gods, the manna, the "What is it?" And your proper garment is your garment of Or, your Meissner field (what science calls it). And literally, it's about a thousand times what you have now.

The amazing thing about superconductors is that they don't have to touch for their energy to flow from one superconductor to another. Electricity has to touch. Superconductors can sit at a distance from each other, as long as they are in resonant frequency *with each other, they are One. They function as one. So when you have your perfect superconducting body, you're not of this space-time. You are a light being, and your mind is one with other people's minds. You literally know their thoughts, and they know your thoughts. You and they are literally of one mind, one heart, and this is science.*

The Bible says that the man who will plant the golden tree of life, which in Hebrew is the ORME tree (the name of my patents — at the time I had no idea of the connection). When my cousin joined the Mormon Church, she had to do their genealogy, and his great, great, great grandmother is Hanah DeVries, daughter of Christopher DeVries, brother of Claude DeVries [see reference 2 above, and Holy Blood, Holy Grail]. Nostradamus worked for the DeVries family, and Nostradamus prophesied that by 1999, the occult gold would be known to science.

The old enemy of religion, the old enemy of philosophy is science, but in fact, science will serve up the confirmation and science will be the one who brings this to the world.

Religion has tried to do this for two thousand years, and it's failed miserably. The world is no darn good. People are no darn good. They're greedy; they're selfish. The Capitalist system has worn out, based on selfishness and greed. But Science can take this to the world in four or five years. Once it is accepted and understood by scientists, the breakthroughs will just be astronomical.

A basic analytical breakthrough. You can fill yourself with this light. In The Dead Sea Scrolls Uncovered, not only did the Qumran community have a metallurgical foundry in the middle of the city, but you also find out that the teacher of righteousness, this thing they were totally preoccupied with, wasn't Moses or Christ. It says the High Priest swallows the teacher of righteousness. The TR is the holy spirit, the TR for those scientists is the light, the zero-point light that isn't measurable. It is, in fact, the light, the god source within us. We know all things. We don't have to read or study. We just know.

When your light body exceeds your material body, you don't have to eat food. You can if you want, but you don't have to. You have perfect telepathy. How much more could you ever be judged than for everyone to know your heart and your mind. Everything about you is known. No more hidden agendas, no more lies, no more deceit. Everything is known. And this is called the opening of the book of light. In Revelations, it says, "Blessed be the man who shall overcome, for he shall be given the hidden manna, the white stone of the purest kind upon which will be written a new name." He will not be the same person. It's encoded in your DNA waiting to be activated.

It says that at 1160 degrees, the white powder of gold fuses to form gold glass. It's a transparent glass, just like window glass.

And in Revelations, it says, "The streets of the New Jerusalem will be paved with gold of the purest light, as transparent as glass, and the foundations of New Jerusalem will be made with gold liken unto glass."

This is the gold glass, the very basis of the New Jerusalem. The very basis of raising our self and our consciousness to this higher state. This highest light that will activate all of our DNA will cause us to use all of our brain again, and we will return again to the original state that we were created to be in. Before we fell to the sleeping existence we know now.

These elements are in all of the herbs, the herbal teas, and many of the vegetables you vegetarians are eating. You get them in small amounts. Through work, dedication, years of study and meditation, you can achieve similar results. But it is tough to be a Tibetan Monk. This is called the Keys of the Kingdom. You insert it, and turn it and... It isn't the answer, but the way to the answer. But if you step through that door, that's your decision. Nobody's going to make you take it.

There are many people in this world that don't want this to happen. But this is the New World Order, just not the one George Bush saw. It can be scary. But it is here. Every piece is now known to Science. The philosophical implications are immense.

END OF THE PRESENTATION OF DAVID HUDSON

Many Christians just accept the stories in the Bible on what can only be described as pure faith. However, it appears that there are actually scientific basis for many of the so-called miracles discussed in this ancient text. For example, there is little doubt that the Hebrews survived on something called Manna during their wondering in the desert. There are numerous Biblical accounts of the use of this Manna, which is said to come from Heaven as a gift of the gods. There are other discussions about this white gold being used to extend human life such as in the case of the Count de Saint-Germaine.

Moses, the Hebrew leader was trained in Egyptian esoteric knowledge, did he know that the Pharaohs took of this powdered gold and lived long healthy lives? There are those who think he did. It would also explain his demand that the people drink the residue of the destruction of the Golden calf the Hebrews constructed while Moses was on the mountain communing with God.

This monatomic gold was also believed to be the famed Philosopher's Stone that alchemists searched for throughout history. Many believe that it was this monatomic gold powder that allowed those patriarchs in the Bible to live unbelievably long lives. If this is true, and we have rediscovered the secret of almost eternal life handed down to us by the sky gods, why don't we use it? One of many questions that those I have discussed this book with have asked. I have no answers, but if what is said about monatomic gold is true, then perhaps it can open the way to eternal health and life. Perhaps once again, man can live to be hundreds of years old and not just 3 score and 10.

CHAPTER FOUR

HOW OLD IS CIVILIZATION ON EARTH?

There Are No Artifacts Older Than 5,000 Years.

If the reader will recall, though the Bible talks at length about Summer and what appears to be a widespread civilization existing before the Biblical flood, Zahi Hawass, former Egyptian minister of state for antiquities affairs and secretary-general of the Supreme Council of Antiquities has stated that there are no artifacts found that date before 5,000 years ago. The implication is that there was no organized civilization predating this period. Thus, for example the Sphinx could not be older than 5,000 years old since these massive structures was built by ordinary humans as tombs for their leaders. Thus speaketh the voice of archaeology, thus the Bible must be wrong. Well, not so fast, let's look a little deeper.

For decades, the archaeology field has believed that human civilization only began after the last ice age. This belief maintains that prior to that time, humans were no more than primitive hunter-gathers who could not form a communal organization or demonstrate any sophisticated abilities.

Even further, it is maintained that it was only after the last glacial period following the melting of the ice sheets that covered much of Europe and North America that or ancestors began to develop agriculture and complex economic and social structures. It is theorized that the first cities did not develop until around 3,500 B.C. in Mesopotamia and Egypt. Therefore, as a prime example, the Sphinx could not be older than 3,500 B.C.[22].

To confound the edicts of the leaders in the field of archaeology, research and exploration in other disciplines have unearthed buried civilizations and discovered submerged cities in many parts of the world. This has revealed an unexpected antiquity of man showing that most academic accounts of the origins of civilization and the cultures of the ancient world are completely inaccurate based as they were on the finds uncovered at archaeological sites around the world.

These recent finds make it very clear that a very sophisticated civilization existed not only long prior to the last glacial period but, even more importantly, prior to the "*Younger Dryas Boundary*" cataclysmic event as well[23].

---

[22] Hawking, M.G., Secrets of the Ancient World: The Occult Powers, 2017.

[23] The *Younger Dryas* is a climatic event that occurred from c. 12,900 to c. 11,700 calendar years ago (BP). It is named after an indicator genus, the alpine-tundra wildflower *Dryas octopetala*, as its leaves are occasionally

The *Younger Dryas Boundary* event occurred circa 10,770 B.C. and is thought to have been caused by the air bursts or impacts of several comets crashing into the Earth, resulting in massive shockwaves and firestorms sweeping across continents and initiating a 1,200 year long epoch of terminal environmental change, including devastating cold, perpetual darkness, massive floods, and catastrophic faunal extinctions. While this unprecedented event may have accounted for the vanishing of an advanced civilization from the pages of history, there are still clues to how wide spread this mysterious civilization may have been.

Even Plato[24] wrote of this mysterious civilization when he discussed his trip to Egypt. He wrote that Egyptian priests kept records of their history going back over 19,000 years. Among these ancient records were accounts of the arrival of the time of *Zep Tepi*, or the first time the bringers of knowledge arrived on the Earth in their cosmic egg radiating colored light. These cosmic eggs came bearing the gods who brought the gift of civilization to Egypt and whose rule over humanity is said to have begun circa

---

abundant in the Late Glacial, often minerogenic-rich, like the lake sediments of **Scandinavian** lakes.

The Younger Dryas impact hypothesis, also known as the Clovis comet hypothesis, is one of the competing scientific explanations for the onset of the Younger Dryas cold period after the last glacial period. The Younger Dryas ice age lasted for about 1,200 years before the climate warmed again.

[24] 428 – 348 B.C.

18,000 B.C.[25]

Contrary to the accepted wisdom that there are no artifacts older than 5,000 years, please consider the following discoveries that contradict the pronouncements of archaeologists. In fact, the following are just a few of the many examples that point to the existence of a mysterious advanced civilization that still exists for scientists and laymen alike to marvel at:

- Gundung Padang (Mountain of Light) is located in Cianjur Regency, West Java Province of Indonesia. This is the site of numerous megaliths including a 300-foot high pyramid whose base materials have been dated to 22,000 to 20,000 B.C.
- On the west bank of the Nile River, there is the Ancient Egyptian Temple of Edfu. On the walls of this ancient Temple are inscriptions that tell of an Egyptian civilization extending back to 18,000 B.C.
- In the Sahara Desert in Southern Egypt, west of Aswan is Nabta Playa, the site of some 25 megalithic structures, including a calendar circle with rather sophisticated astronomical alignments, estimated by research teams to have been built as early as 16,500 B.C.
- Puma Punku means the Door of the Puma. This site located

---

[25] The texts inscribed on the walls of the Temple of Edfu contain explicit descriptions of the time of Zep Tepi and the arrival of the sky gods.

in the Andean Mountains in western Bolivia at *Tiwanaku* is a site of incredibly precise stonework. These extensive megalithic structures have astronomical alignments dated to 15,000 B.C. and represent construction practices far too sophisticated to have been built by the primitive society envisioned by most historians.

- Probably one of the most famous of these ancient sites is Gobekli Tepe, located in the southeastern Anatolia Region of Turkey, northeast of Sanliurfa. This complex megalithic site is dated to have flourished from 12,000 to 9,000 B.C.

- The Great Sphinx is located on the Giza Plateau adjacent to the west bank of the Nile in Giza, Egypt. In spite of Zahi Hawass objections, the weathering and erosion patters correlated with the paleoclimatology and subsurface features to establish that the body of the Sphinx and the walls of its enclosure date to the period of 11,000 to 7,000 B.C.

- On the Arabian Sea Coast of India, bordering the state of Gujarat, in the Bay of Cambay or Gulf of Khambhat as some call it, there is a vast submerged city sold old that there are not even legends about its builders. Artifacts that have come from the ruins have been carbon dated to 9,500 B.C.

- Offshore of the westernmost inhabited island of Japan,

located some 108 KM from the East Coast of Taiwan lies the underwater complex of Yonaguni. This site is estimated to have submerged beneath the sea circa 10,000 to 8,000 B.C.

- Finally, there is the sunken city of Dwarka located offshore of the Devbhoomi Dwarka district in the state of Gujarat, in northwestern India. This site is massive, rivaling modern cities in both size and sophistication of construction. Relics from the ruins have been carbon dated to 7,000 B.C.

There is much that we do not know about the history of the human race or even the development of the Homo sapiens as a species for that matter. But for purposes of this work, for example, consider the following questions:

- How did the Sumerian Civilization, fully developed, just appear out of nowhere some 6,000 years ago?
- Who were the Sumerians?
- Where did they get that unusually advanced knowledge that they demonstrated in so many fields?
- Why did their civilization just vanish?

Though there have been unknown civilizations found throughout the world, what is known to history as ancient Sumer, only discovered in Mesopotamia a scant 150 years ago, seems to be oldest civilization on record. As referenced above it just appeared fully developed, rose to great heights and then as a civilization just vanished. Based on our history as taught in our universities this is absolutely impossible.

Sumer was the first known great civilization in history[26]. It was located between the Tigris and the Euphrates Rivers at the headwaters of the Persian Gulf. Sumer was known in Biblical times as Chaldea or Shinar. Today, we all know of this region as Iraq, which even obtained its name from the ancient Sumerian city of Uruk.

Before this mysterious civilization vanished its teachings and influence had spread as far to the east as the Indus River and down to the Nile River. Its teachings helped shape later civilizations well into the future. It actually handed down the basics for all ensuring western civilizations from language to mathematics, agriculture and astronomy.

Amazingly, nothing was known about this mother of all civilizations until about 150 years ago when archeologists began to excavate the strange mounds that dotted the countryside of Southern Iraq. The earliest contemporary mention of the possibility of a lost civilization actually came from the writings of Pietro Della Valle[27], an Italian composer, musicologist and author who

---

[26] Marrs, Jim, The Illuminati: The Secret Society that Hijacked the World, Visible Ink Press, Detroit, MI (2017)

[27] Pietro Della Valle was born in Rome, Italy April 2, 1586 to a very wealthy family. After an unfortunate love affair that ended badly, he was advised by a professor of medicine from Naples to travel and it was suggested that he travel east. While in the Middle East he made one of the first modern

traveled throughout Asia during the Renaissance period. He explored the Holy Land, the Middle East, and North Africa and even ventured as far as India.

In 1843, a Frenchman by the name of Paul-Emile Botta discovered the ruins of the palace of Sargon II near modern day Khorsabad. Soon after other early archaeologists found buried cities, broken palaces, artifacts, and an unbelievable number of clay tablets that described every facet of Sumerian life. By the late 1800s and early 1900s, Sumerian had been recognized as an original language and was being translated by scholar. However, the general public is still not being educated on the importance of this early civilization.

Over 500,000 of the clay tablets upon which Sumerians kept their records have ben found but only a small fraction (less than 20%) has been translated. Not to let a little thing like new facts disturb their outdated theories, histories have stuck to their guns, maintaining that Sumer grew out of a collection of hunter-gatherer clans who banded together to form the first human civilization in the Tigris-Euphrates River Valley about 4,000[28] B.C.E.

---

records of the location of Babylon. He also brought back inscribed bricks from Ninevah and Ur. His writings were the spur that brought Archaeologists to the area containing Sumer.

[28] It must be remembered that no less a leader in he field of archaeology, Zahi Hawass, has categorically stated that there have been no artifacts that pre-date 5,000 years ago.

Archaeologists have conducted digs that have shown that by 3300 B.C.E. the Sumerians had developed an amazingly advanced civilization that included draining marshes, development of a very complicated of lengthy canal dams and dikes and they had built a large scale irrigation system.

Historians have recognized that Sumer was the first urban civilization in the historical region of southern Mesopotamia during the early Bronze Age. The earliest written texts come from the cities of Uruk ad Jemdet Nasr and date back to 3,300 B.C. No one knows for sure when Sumer was settled, but it is theorized by modern historians it was first settled between circa 5,500 and 4,000 B.C. by a West Asian people who spoke the Sumerian language.

A rich and fertile kingdom is a target so it was that by 2,400 B.C.E. Sumer was invaded and captured by King Sargon the Great who founded the Semite Akkadian dynasty which stretched from the Persian Gulf to the Mediterranean Sea. After a number of years of warfare, the lands that had comprised the ancient civilization of Sumer were united under Hammurabi of Babylon[29].

By conquering what had been ancient Sumer and Sargon's Akkadian dynasty, Hammurabi became ruler of a vast number of people moving to what they perceived as a safe located as a result of wars and geophysical catastrophes. It is only recently, that it has

---

[29] Hammurabi of Babylon issued what became known to history as Hammurabi's Code a system of laws that has been praised for eons as a first step in developing a more advanced legal system.

become clear that the famous Hammurabi's Code was actually based on a series of laws drafted by the Sumerians centuries prior to Hammurabi. The Sumerian legal code plagiarized by Hammurabi was probably the earliest legal code yet discovered. The Sumerian King Ur-Nammu laid down this very early legal system.

It was not just in the field of law that Sumerians excelled. This early civilization also gave us mathematics based on a sexagesimal system [30], which permitted a precise method of measuring large quantities by area and volume. This system was used by the Babylonians and is still in use today. This base 60 system was used to measure time [31], angles and geographic coordinates.

Their knowledge of astronomy was nothing short of amazing. As observed by Alan Alford in his book *Gods of the New Millennium: Scientific Proof of Flesh and Blood Gods*[32], the whole concept of spherical astronomy, including the 360 degree circle, the zenith, the horizon, the celestial axis, the poles, the ecliptic, the equinoxes and much more all rose suddenly in Sumer. It was Sumerian knowledge of the movements of the sun and the moon

---

[30] This is a numerical system based on 60.
[31] Check your watch.
[32] Alford, Alan, Gods of the Millennium: Scientific proof of Flesh and Blood Gods, Hodder and Stoughton, June 1999.

that resulted in the world's first calendar, used for centuries by the Semites, Egyptians, Greeks and others.

Many would be surprised that the Biblical Patriarch Abraham was of Sumerian birth, a Sumerian nobleman from Ur of Chaldea (ancient Iraq)[33] and along with the Army he led out of Sumer brought the knowledge of Sumer to Egypt by means of codes found within the Torah and other old Hebraic text such as the Book of Creation and the Book of Light.

Even with all of this knowledge, the question still remains: how did early humans of almost 6,000 years ago transform themselves from small clans of hunter-gatherers into a full blown civilization that would be considered advanced even by today's standards? Historians have wondered about this for decades and arrived no closer to the answer than they were at the beginning. Of course, the best way to find out how a civilization achieved some advancement is to ask that civilization, but when the answer does not tally with the desires of the questioner, the answer is written off as myth or legend, for you see, Sumer itself has answered the question as to how they achieved their greatness as we will discuss.

In the thousands of Sumerian tablets that have been translated, the Sumerians themselves have answered this very question. According to their answer, they state that everything that they achieved came from beings that came down from the sky.

---

[33] Confirmed by Biblical texts.

According to Zacharia Sitchin, all of the ancient people spoke of being visited by gods who descended to earth from the heavens. However, scholars, who call them myths, have discounted these stories. Sitchin also pointed out that he believes it is significant that the Sumerians never originally referred to these beings as gods but did hold them in reverence[34] as the Annunaki or those who came from the heavens to the Earth.

Historians also think of the ancient empires of the Sumerians, Babylonians, Akkadians, Phoenicians and Assyrians as separate empires, but according to Sitchin this is wrong. Each of these empires was a watered down version of its predecessor, each being less advanced that that which came before it. Modern wisdom would believe that the new civilization would be the most advanced, but in this case it is the reverse. How did ancient Sumer reach such great heights only to fall so far and then eventually vanish into the sands of time?

It should also be known that within the Sumerian tablets were references to many astounding scientific and technological references that these ancient people could have absolutely developed no concept of without outside influence. Among the topics discussed in these ancient tablets were such concepts as genetic engineering, cloning, interplanetary travel, instantaneous

---

[34] It was the Romans and the Greeks who called these beings gods and they fashioned their own deities after the Sumerians' sky peoples.

distant communication and the use of what were referred to as techno-magical chips (MEs) which were translated as formulas before Sitchin introduced the concept a of high tech civilization interacting with these ancient peoples.

Ben Franklin Was Not the First

Unusual discoveries that would tend to upset the apple cart so to speak will get Archaeologists out in droves to discredit the new finds. A case in point is what was referred to as The Baghdad Battery or the Parthian Battery. This discovery is a set of three artifacts, which were found together: a ceramic pot, a tube of one metal, and a rod of another. It was discovered in modern Khujut Rabu[35], Iraq, close to the metropolis of Ctesiphon, the capital of Parthian (150 BC-223 AD) or Sasanian (224-650 AD) empires, and it is considered to date back to either periods.

In spite of its clear use to generate an electrical current, archaeologist argue that this unusual artifact's origin and purpose remain unclear, and further evidence is needed to explain its purpose. It was hypothesized by some researchers that the object functioned as a **galvanic cell**, possibly used for electroplating, or

---

[35] Khujut Rabu' is a local area to the South-East of Baghdad, Iraq, near the town of the present-day Salman Pak. Also Khujut Rabua. In ancient times this was the location of Ctesiphon and Seleucia on the Tigris. This area was the capital city of the Parthian Civilization. Modern excavations of these two ancient cites have provided many artifacts from ancient times, including the alleged Baghdad Battery. Modern tourists can still visit the Arch of Ctesiphon.

some kind of electrotherapy; but there is no electro-gilded object known to exist from this period. It has been suggested that an alternative explanation is that they functioned as storage vessels for sacred scrolls.

The artifacts consist of terracotta pots approximately 130 mm (5 in) tall (with a one-and-a-half-inch mouth) containing a cylinder made of a rolled copper sheet, which houses a single iron rod. At the top, the iron rod is isolated from the copper by bitumen, with plugs or stoppers, and both rod and cylinder fit snugly inside the opening of the jar. The copper cylinder is not watertight, so if the jar were filled with a liquid, this would surround the iron rod as well. The artifact had been exposed to the weather and had suffered corrosion.

Wilhelm König [36] thought the objects might date to the Parthian period, between 250 BC and AD 224, but according to St John Simpson of the Near Eastern department of the British Museum, their original excavation and context were not well-recorded, and evidence for this date range is very weak. Furthermore, the style of the pottery is Sassanid (224-640).

Most of the components of the objects are not particularly amenable to advanced dating methods. The ceramic pots could be analyzed by thermo-luminescence dating, but this has not yet been

---

[36] Wilhelm König was an assistant at the National Museum of Iraq in the 1930s.

done; in any case, it would only date the firing of the pots, which is not necessarily that of the complete artifact.

In 1938 Wilhelm König authored a paper offering the hypothesis that they may have formed a galvanic cell, perhaps used for electroplating gold onto silver objects. This theory was immediately rejected, out of hand, by skeptics who believe that no one in this time period could possibly have had any idea about the generation of electricity or even had any idea what electricity was. Leading the mass of skeptics was, naturally, a large number of archaeologists, because after all, they didn't think of it so it could not be true. However, with al of the doubters, it would see that no one tried to use the artifacts to try and generate any current.

Some who believe in the battery theory thing that wine, lemon juice, grape juice, or vinegar was used as an acidic electrolyte solution to generate an electric current from the difference between the electrode potentials of the copper and iron electrodes. König had observed a number of very fine silver objects from ancient Iraq, plated with very thin layers of gold, and speculated that they were electroplated using batteries with these as the cells.

After the Second World War, a man named Willard Gray demonstrated current production by a reconstruction of the inferred battery design when filled with grape juice. W. Jansen experimented with benzoquinone (some beetles produce quinones) and vinegar in a cell and got satisfactory performance.

In 1978, Arne Eggebrecht reportedly reproduced the electroplating of gold onto a small statue. There are no (direct) written or photographic records of this experiment. The only records are segments of a television show where the experiment was filmed. Since this experiment was not presented the proper way (the way of the archaeologist) it was not accepted by the scientific world.

So this discovery which could have opened the way into an avenue of research that could have yielded unbelievable discoveries. However, archaeologists and other "scientists, using their age old motto of "the idea didn't come from us and can't be true" stopped any deeper research into what these items might have been.

It would seem that most mainstream research focused on what these items were not rather than what they might have been. Among the other objections raised by archaeologists were"

- König himself seems to have been mistaken on the nature of the objects he thought were electroplated. They were apparently fire-gilded (with mercury). Paul Craddock of the British Museum said "*The examples we see from this region and era are conventional gold plating and mercury gilding. There's never been any irrefutable evidence*[37] *to support the electroplating theory".*

- David A. Scott, senior scientist at the Getty Conservation Institute and head of its Museum Research Laboratory, wrote that "*There is a natural tendency for writers dealing with chemical technology to envisage these unique ancient objects of two thousand years ago as electroplating accessories (Foley 1977) but this is clearly untenable, for there is absolutely no evidence for electroplating in this region at the time.*"

- Paul T. Keyser of the University of Alberta noted that Eggebrecht used a more efficient, modern electrolyte, and that using only vinegar, or other electrolytes available at the time assumed, the battery would be very feeble, and for that and other reasons concludes that even if this was in fact a battery, it could not have been used for electroplating. However, Keyser still supported the battery theory, but believed it was used for some kind of mild electrotherapy such as pain relief, possibly through electro-acupuncture.

It is interesting to note that the items in question were among those objects looted along with thousands of other artifacts

---

[37] Since he spoke of irrefutable evidence, clearly there was evidence, but the leaders of the field decided it was not conclusive. So much for the open scientific mind.

from the National Museum during the 2003 invasion of Iraq. As this looting has been described as planed and very carefully carried out with military precision, cold some group have not wanted any research into the use of electricity in the far distant past?

In March 2012, Professor Elizabeth Stone of Stony Brook University, an expert on Iraqi archaeology, returning from the first archaeological expedition in Iraq after 20 years, stated that she does not know a single archaeologist who believed that these were batteries. So that ends the discussion, the wise leaders in the field of archaeology do not believe that these items represented batteries, so without any modern examination, they were not batteries, problem solved.

CHAPTER FIVE

THERE WERE GIANTS IN THOSE DAYS

As children we have our heads filled with nursery rhymes, stories of dragons and giants. As we grow older, we are told that all of these stories are just make believe, there are no dragons and certainly there are no giants. Those in the mainstream disciplines such as archaeologists and geologists are loath to discuss those things outside their belief system.

For example, while getting my first degree (I have 5) I asked my geology professor how he explained giant footprints that had been found in strata or those anomalies such as machined artifacts being dug up from deep within the earth. He just shrugged and said some are hoaxes and others are flukes hardly worth examining. In other words, if it is outside our knowledge, lets not disturb things by trying to fit these oddities into our knowledge base. Hardly the words of a true scientist.

I have spoken earlier about mainstream scientists, such as archaeologist suppressing theories that are not in keeping with the accepted way of looking at things, but now we are going to look at examples of hiding finds that tend to cast doubt on that sacred belief, Darwin's Theory of Evolution[38].

---

[38] For those that believe that Darwin's Theory of Evolution is a proven scientific fact, it is not. Even Darwin speculated about a supposed missing

JUST WHO WERE OUR ANCESTERS?

It will, I am sure, amaze the reader to find out that at least one race of giants inhabited Europe and much of the Americas at least up until the time of the Spanish Conquistadors. Their graves have been found in many parts of North America, and the records left behind by the earliest explorers confirm their existence. However, whenever these skeletons are found that do not fit in with accepted theories of evolution, representatives of the Smithsonian Institute show up and the evidence is taken "for study" only to vanish and never been seen again. But do not take my word for it; let's look at some examples.

We live in a time where young and old both have tremendous amounts of data available at their fingertips through the electronic Internet. Yet in this literal tsunami of information, certain areas are literally off limits, among them the truth about the early history of the human race. The sad truth is that the true ancient history of man is based on an unproven theory that is protected to the point of there being a worldwide archaeological cover-up to protect the what might be looked at as the status quo. A prime example of this orchestrated effort to suppress discoveries that would bring everything we know about the history of the human race deals with the topic of giants. Every ancient culture

---

link that would explain the jump from primate to Homo Sapien. It has never been found, however, most anthropologists and archaeologists treat the writing of Darwin as something close to the Ten Commandments.

has stories and records detailing their interactions with giant humanoids, but the very idea that such giant creatures lived in relatively recent times, is laughed at by the mainstream media and so-called real scientists.

Not only the Holy Bible, but also numerous other religious texts speak of these giants but the very idea has been relegated to the realm of fantasy. Unfortunately for mainstream archaeologists, there are new discoveries revealing the existence of new species of humans that have popped up periodically. As an example in 2012, discoveries in southwest China brought to light the existence of what are called the Red Cave Deer People[39]. How many other unknown species of Humans lie hidden beneath the ground?

Then in the early part of 2015, fishermen of the coast of Taiwan discovered a 4-inch fossilized human jawbone belonging to a new kind of primitive human that once inhabited Southeast Asia over 190,000 years ago. This new species was christened Penghu man after the island chain near where the bones were found[40]. Research was conclusive that these fossilized bones bore no relation to Peking Man or Java Man, rather it represented a heretofore unknown primitive race. It was also confirmed that this

---

[39] *"Red Deer Cave People Bone Points to Mysterious Species of Pre-Modern Human."* Science Daily. University of New South Wales, December 17, 2015.
[40] Ryall, Julian, *"Fishermen Discover Fossil From New Type of Primitive Human."* Telegraph. January 28, 2015.

newly discovered cousin of Homo Sapien was not related to the mysterious "Hobbit Race" known as Homo floresiensis[41].

Speaking of newly discovered species, the problem for mainstream scientists such as archaeologists is that they do not fit neatly into the historical timeline carefully worked out by the leaders in the scientific world. After all, who would ever believe that a race of Hobbits would be found in the real world, these little people are the stuff of legends and movies, not the real world. However, with a few strings being pulled, these major discoveries are not front-page matters, but relegated to the inner pages of the world's press. Another problem defused, archaeological theories are safe once more.

Unfortunately, the real world has its own timeline, not one artificially created by leaders in some discipline. More unknown species of human have been found and unsettling information has been found about those previously unknown species already found.

Research into the species referred to as Hobbits has revealed that they existed as recently as 12,000 years ago. It is interesting to note that this is the same time period in which the pre-flood world came to an end and the cataclysmic events of the Ice Age began. These discoveries should have sent archaeologists

---

[41] Castro, Joseph, *"Homo Floresiensis: Facts About the Hobbit."* Live Science. January 15, 2016.

scurrying off to delve deeper into the history of the mysterious Hobbits, but instead it was business as usual.

It is also very clear that the natural disasters that disrupted life on this planet and apparently put an end to the Hobbits also matched the extinctions of a number of other human species such as the Neanderthals and the Denisovans.

But, there were still more discoveries that threatened the sanctity of accepted archaeological thought. Take for instance the H. Naledi discovered in 2015. This species was a race of dwarfs similar to the Hobbits that was discovered deep inside a South African cave. These bones were dated to at least 500,000 years ago [42].

As if this was not bad enough for accepted thought, there was the discovery of Homo rudolfensis [43]. This species was discovered in Kenya in the 1970s and the dating of their bones found them to date from 1.9 million years ago, long before archaeology has said that humans, as such, existed. What does this do to the sacred Theory of Evolution? How can archaeologists ignore these findings? Easily, they just ignore them.

Well, while mainstream science was wrestling with these questions, a team of archaeologists made another discovery in the

---

[42] Shreeve, Jaime, *"This Face Changes The Human Story. But How?"* National Geographic. September 10, 2015.
[43] Benton, Adam, *"Homo Rudolfensis: Finally Shown To Be A Separate Species?"* Evoanth. August 12, 2012.

Afar region of Ethiopia in 2015. This discovery consisted of hominin jawbones and teeth belonging to an unknown race of humans[44] dating back 3.5 million years ago[45]. This particular find made it clear that this species was living at the same time as the Australopithecus family, including the world famous "Lucy". An examination of her bones showed that she was alive and well 3 to 3.8 million years ago. So it would appear that the planet was rather populated some 3,000,000 years ago.

Of course, then there is the most mysterious heretofore, unknown race of all, the Denisovans. Research has revealed that the Denisovans were a cousin of the Neanderthals who intermingled with Homo sapiens over 60,000 years ago. However, what is most puzzling about the research that has been conducted in regard to this unknown race is that the genomes of the Denisovans contain a segment of DNA that comes from another species completely unknown to science.

The DNA testing revealed that the Denisovans mated with a mystery species from Asia that is neither human nor Neanderthal and had huge giant-like teeth[46]. As icing on the case, so to speak, archaeologists also found four expertly crafted hunting spears that

---

[44] This race has been dubbed Australopithecus deyiremeda, which means close relative in the language of the Afar people.
[45] Morelle, Rebecca, "*New Species of Ancient Human Found.*" BBC. May 28, 2015.
[46] Gresko, Michael, "*DNA Reveals Mysterious Human Cousins With Huge Teeth.*" National Geographic. November 16, 2015.

date back over 400,000 years. These spears are considered the oldest and most complete hunting weapons ever discovered. However, in spite of this very concrete evidence that Humans, of one shape form or fashion were hunting over 400,000 years ago, the evidence was ignored by mainstream academia since the Darwinian model makes it clear that humans did not begin hunting until about 40,000 years ago.

Advances in DNA research also threaten of the long cherished beliefs of academia. Recent research has revealed that human carry more than 145 "alien" genes that have no direct link to our ancestors. This makes it very clear that evolution does not rely solely on genes passed down through the ages[47]. Scientists discovered that mathematical codes in our DNA cannot be explained by evolution and some researchers have even suggested that our "junk DNA" is the result of a genetic engineering experiment conducted by an alien race millions of years ago.

Proof of these experiments might be found in the elongated skulls discovered in the Paracas region of Peru. DNA testing of these unusual skulls confirmed that they had mitochondrial DNA with mutations unknown in any human, primate or any other

---

[47] Prigg, Mark, *"Mystery of Our 145 "Alien " Genes: Scientists Discover Some DNA Is Not From Out Ancestor and Say It Could Change How We Think About Evolution."* Daily Mail. March 13, 2015.

animal for that matter. It is also interesting to note that these unusual skulls were discovered with heads full of red hair[48].

So now we have evidence supporting the existence of a number of new species that were previously unknown to science. We also have proof that there was another, still unknown race that interbreeded with early man to produce what can only be referred to as hybrids. Who were these hybrids and where did they go? These questions have never been answered, but perhaps we can get a glimmer of an answer as we move forward.

COLUMBUS WAS A LATE COMER

As I progressed through school one of my favorite subjects was history. I was fascinated by the history of the world, but most importantly, the history of the United States and North America. While I was introduced to this topic over 55 years ago, one thing I clearly remember was that it was a sacred tenet of history that prior to the arrival of Christopher Columbus in 1492, there were a few wandering tribes on the North American Continent and their ancestors came across that convenient land bridge in the Bering Strait. To suggest otherwise was to risk a failing grade, not matter what evidence you might have been able to marshal to support your idea.

---

[48] Forester, Brien, "*DNA Tests Results: Paracas Skulls Are Not Human.*" Ancient Code. December 26, 2015.

Well, even that concept is now in jeopardy of being proven wrong. We now know that the Vikings had a presence what is now the northeast United States and southern Canada, there is evidence that ancient Chinese made voyages to the west coast of North America and the Romans built a city in Arizona during the time of Nero and in 1,000 AD there was a civilization called the Cahokia Culture in western Illinois, across the Mississippi River from where St. Louis, Missouri now stands. However, there are no discussions in academia about these ancient inhabitants.

In fact, research has shown that in 1,000 AD the population of Cahokia was estimated to be greater than that of London, England[49]. In fact, Cahokia as the capital of a commercial empire that stretched from the upper Great Lakes to the Gulf of Mexico. Cahokia also served as a hub of an even great network of cities. This was called the Mississippian culture, which consisted of a confederation of pyramid builders that dominated North America east of the Mississippi River. Unfortunately, this thriving culture collapsed about 100 years before the arrival of Columbus.

Delving deeply into what historical research has been conducted regarding ancient North America reveals some very startling information. The first organized civilization on the North American Continent of which there is any mention is the Adena

---

[49] Joseph, Frank, <u>Advanced Civilizations of Prehistoric America</u>, Bear & Company, Rochester, Vermont, 2010.

who appear to have arrived in the Ohio Valley with a fully developed civilization about 1,000 BC. The Adena culture spread out to cover the area between the Atlantic coast and the Mississippi River. For over 1,700 years, their achievements ranged from building massive earthworks and hill forts to accomplishing complicated dental procedures to developing a distinctive style of pottery. They were also the first inhabitants of the North American continent to practice organized agriculture until their sudden disappearance as a distinctive culture about 700 AD.

Some of their achievements can be found in Rock Lake at Lake Mills, Wisconsin. A pyramidal structure, the Winnebago Indians call the Temple of the Moon, was constructed by the Adena approximately 3,000 years ago. A very early period for a society to have developed a social infrastructure to accomplish something like this, but James Scherz, professor of surveying and environmental studies at the university of Wisconsin at Madison is adamant that his dating of the structure was correct[50].

About the year 300 BC, the Hopewell culture sprouted in the Ohio Valley. They built massive ceremonial centers, the first known highway system and developed a trading empire that imported goods from the Gulf of Mexico to the Canadian shores of

---

[50] Joseph, Frank, Advanced Civilizations of Prehistoric America, Bear & Company, Rochester, Vermont, 2010.

the Great Lakes. However, even this massive, powerful culture came to an end. It collapsed suddenly about 400 AD.

For some 200 hundred years after the end of these mighty civilizations, there was little effort to form any new civilization. However, the Cahokia Culture sprang up throughout the Mississippi Valley and reached unbelievable heights until the collapse of this civilization about 1300 AD.

At the same time, the Hohokam and Anasazi cultures were designing and building truly vast and sophisticated irrigation networks across the Southwest. However, they too simply vanished into the sands of time, simply walking off and abandoning their huge sophisticated cities.

HISTORICAL BREAD CRUMBS

Many of the stories about Giants in North America seem to have spread from the Bronze Age copper traders that once roamed the upper Midwest. For those not a student of history, what is called the Bronze Age was a period in our history that saw widespread use of bronze from about 3,200 – 600 BC. Archaeologists and other historians have spun many theories about this time period without coming up with an answer to explain one question. Where did all of the copper required to make the Bronze used extensively during this time period come from? The only possible answer is America.

It has been determined that an unbelievable amount of copper was mined in the Midwest during the European Bronze Age. However, no one knows what happened to all of that copper. When asked if it could have been exported to Europe mainstream archaeologists always answer with a resounding no as they are adamant that there was no transoceanic contact between the Old World and New World during the Bronze Age. This in spite of the body of evidence showing that the best copper of the era couldn't have come from Europe.

From a Bronze Age shipwreck off the coast of Turkey came over 10 tons of copper oxide ingots of an unbelievably purity, 99.5%. Only Michigan Copper, which was mined in enormous amounts during the Bronze Age, is of this purity. These ingots were also found in Crete, Sardinia, Cyprus, Turkey, Bulgaria, Israel, Egypt and England. While copper is one of the most common metals in the world, copper that registers over 90 percent pure is extremely rare and has only been discovered in the copper mines of the American Midwest. Historians believe that over a half a billion pounds of copper was mined by ancient miners and literally vanished. No one has any idea where this copper went.

However, the Native American tribes that inhabited that region claim that the copper was mined by a race of sea-going red-haired giants. It is interesting that other than evidence of their mining operation, this race of giants left no other evidence of their existence.

In 1924, a pair of bat guano farmers discovered a group of mummified giants buried with fishnets, duck decoys and shell art in a cave in Lovelock, Nevada. Clearly, these giants dated from a period of time when what we know as Nevada was crisscrossed by tremendous rivers, lakes and other water sources [51]. A giant handprint and 15 inch sandals were also found in the cave, though a concerted effort has been made to remove the giant handprint. The local Paiutes have oral traditions that tell of a race of unfriendly, cannibalistic, redheaded giants that came to the Lovelock cave area from an unknown land thousands of years ago [52].

There is evidence that these red headed giants explored the American West over 3,000 years before the travels of the Mountain Men and Lewis and Clark. It also seems that they were very observant in regard to the flora and fauna. A shrub typically found in the rainforest of the Pacific Northwest and that does not appear any place else east of the Mississippi was brought to the Lake Superior region in Ancient times and planted in the environs of the ancient copper mines. The unique thing about this particular

---

[51] Haze, Xaviant, Ancient Giants of the Americas, New Page Books, Wayne, New Jersey, 2017.
[52] Hill, Bryan, "Lovelock Cave: A Tale of Giants or a Giant Tale of Fiction?" Ancient Origins. May 15, 2015.

plant was that it has been used medicinally for hundreds of years to treat diabetes, tumors and tuberculosis. Someone was planning ahead and clearly had the organizational skills to send an expedition across the country to get this very beneficial plant and bring it back to the mining region. At a time when archaeologists claims that a few primitive Indians were wandering around this massive continent, clearly there were other unknown entities at work with skills far beyond what we have been led to believe. Let's see who they might be.

CHAPTER SIX

MORE EVIDENCE THAT THERE WERE GIANTS IN THOSE DAYS

It is rather clear that the history of North American is not what we have been told it was. There were at least four rather advanced civilizations that made this continent their home until they mysteriously collapsed. Now let's go a step further and see if we can find any concrete evidence that there were actual giants living in North America in pre-history.

LOST CITY IN THE GRAND CANYON

There is an old, old story that Egyptians crossed the Pacific Ocean and wandered the American Southwest thousands of years ago leaving behind a tomb of one of their leaders. Those who subscribe to this ancient tale point to an odd story out of Arizona. In the early 20th century, claims of such a discovery were made by two Smithsonian-funded archaeologists, who spoke of a thriving civilization tucked within a series of caverns carved into the side of a remote portion of the Grand Canyon.

According to the story, while rafting down the river, one of the men spotted what appeared to be a carving on the side of a sheer cliff. Further exploration showed that the cared area was actually the entrance to a tunnel.

There was a story on the front page of the April 5, 1909

edition of the Arizona Gazette that recounted the discovery of a series of bizarre caves and artifacts in the Marble Canyon region of the Grand Canyon. The report claimed two Smithsonian-funded archaeologists, Prof. S. A. Jordan and G.E. Kinkaid, were responsible for the find. According to the article, this discovery almost conclusively prove that the race which inhabited this mysterious cavern, hewn in solid rock by human hands, was of oriental origin, possibly from Egypt, tracing back to the time of the Pharaoh Ramses.

If their theories are borne out by the translation of the tablets engraved with hieroglyphics, the mystery of the prehistoric peoples of North America, their ancient arts, who they were and whence they came, will be solved. Egypt and the Nile, and Arizona and the Colorado will be linked by a historical chain running back to into the furthest reaches of time.

Later in the article, another discovery is mentioned, a cross-legged idol resembling Buddha was carefully described along with a large tomb filled with mummified humans: a veritable mash-up of Egyptian and East Asian cultures.

The area of this discovery is a dangerous region to explore Although this remote area of the Grand Canyon makes for perilous traveling, expeditions by private collectors and academics went forward. The site of Kincaid's discovery was roughly 42 miles away from El Tovar Crystal Canyon, and the

Arizona Gazette article noted that the cavern's entrance was 1500 feet down a sheer cliff. This is not the easiest terrain to cover, but it's topography that could be overcome today.

Conspiracy theorist John Rhodes claims to know the exact location of the caverns — the site is guarded today by a lone soldier carrying an M-16 and that the caverns are a museum for civilization's shadowy elites. To make things even more bizarre, David Icke connects Kincaid's Grand Canyon discovery with reptilian overlords in his 1999 book The Biggest Secret.

Naturally, the Smithsonian insists that no records exists of Kincaid or Professor Jordan within the Smithsonian's Department of Anthropology, nor is there a paper trail at the Smithsonian detailing the artifacts gathered on the expedition. When asked directly about Kincaid's claims, a Smithsonian Institute representative once said: Well, the first thing I can tell you, before we go any further, is that no Egyptian artifacts of any kind have ever been found in North or South America. Therefore, I can tell you that the Smithsonian Institute has never been involved in any such excavations.

According to conspiracy theorists, the Smithsonian Institute went so far as to destroy artifacts to maintain this historical viewpoint. Espousers of this theory mention man-made mounds with plaster walls strewn across the American Midwest and a series of fire-hewn coffins found in Alabama in 1892 that were turned over the Smithsonian Institute, only to be lost in the years following.

So is the Smithsonian telling the truth when it insists that there is no evidence of Egyptian artifacts being found in North or South America? The reader should judge as we present the next information.

EARLY EXPEDITIONS TO AMERICA

While these next two items do not confirm the existence of giants, they do point to the fact that there is a lot we do not known about our history. The Roman Empire was the direct cause of two little known expeditions to the New World.

The first resulted in a Roman colony that was established near Tucson, Arizona and the second left behind a mysterious southern Illinois treasure that rivaled that of King Tut. This second expedition was to bury King Juba of Mauretania and his treasure in a spot that would be safe from Roman soldiers.

ARIZONA

The discovery had caused much argument and name calling. The existence of this unknown colony was brought to light by the discovery of what are called the Tucson artifacts, sometimes called the Tucson Lead Crosses, Tucson Crosses, Silverbell Road artifacts, or Silverbell artifacts, were thirty-one lead objects that Charles E. Manier and his family found in 1924 near Picture Rocks, Arizona which were initially thought by some to be created by early Mediterranean civilizations that had crossed the Atlantic in the first century, but were later determined to be a hoax by mainstream archaeologists primarily because "we all know it could not be real".

The find comprised thirty-one lead objects consisting of crosses, swords, and religious/ceremonial paraphernalia, most of which contained Hebrew or Latin engraved inscriptions, pictures of temples, leaders' portraits, angels, and a dinosaur (inscribed on the lead blade of a sword). One contained the phrase "Calalus, the unknown land" which was used by believers as the name of the settlement. The objects also have Roman numerals ranging from 790 to 900 inscribed on them, which were sometimes interpreted to represent the date of their creation because the numerals were followed by the letters AD. The site contains no other artifacts, no pottery shards, no broken glass, no human or animal remains, and no sign of hearths or housing, which actually proves nothing but were red flags to skeptical archaeologists.

Then we have the finds in southern Illinois of the tomb of King Juba. The finder, wanting to profit form his discoveries has been very cautious about allowing scientific investigation into the contents of the tomb. However, those few items that have been examined appear to be authentic and date from the time period of the uprising against the Romans by the Mauretanians under the command of King Juba.

However, these two momentous discoveries were naturally suppressed by mainstream science, usually with the help of the Smithsonian Institute. However, there are many more discoveries that call into question everything we think we know about history in North America that demonstrate a pattern of opposition by mainstream science that we should keep in mind in regard to their pronouncements.

INDIAN MOUNDS

Across the country there are numerous massive mounds of earth that have been labeled as Indian Mounds. Even though, in may cases, the local tribes deny all knowledge of these structures, mainstream scientists merely smile condescendingly at how much the tribes have forgotten about their own history. The scientist clearly knows more than a semi-educated Indian if the attitude. However, the evidence supports the beliefs of the Native Americans that their tribes did not build the mounds.

Even first-hand accounts by early settlers to this country that finds that they made in the mysterious mounds supported the premise that there were pre-Columbian voyages, were discounted by mainstream archaeologists as poppycock. As an example, the Governor of Connecticut in 1657, John Winthrop, Jr.[53], a prominent member of the Royal Academy in London wrote

---

[53] Winthrop, John, *A Journal of the Transactions and Occurrences in the Settlement of Massachusetts and the Other New England Colonies From the Year 1630 to 1644*, (Hartford, Conn.: Elisha Babcock, 1790)

extensively about the ancient stone forts and dolmens of New England and compared them to similar structures in southwest England. However, when the history books were written, all of his first hand accounts were left out of the history books since *we all knew* that there was no pre-Columbian contact between the Old World and the New World.

Many of the mysterious mounds in the Ohio Valley were excavated in the late 1800s, sometimes for treasure hunting, sometimes for academic endeavors and sometimes to remove them to gain more farmable land. Whatever may have been the reason, the end result was usually the same, discoveries that literally boggled the mind. Some of these finds consisted of giant skeletons, huge rusty iron helmets, 39 pound copper axes and unique seashell necklaces imported from the Atlantic Ocean.

In Bainbridge, Ohio, excavations revealed mummified bodies wearing pearl covered robes containing over half a million fresh water pearls as well as a number of giant skeletons wearing copper armor to include detailed copper helmets.

A very influential "scientist", J.W. Powell, collected many of the stories of these finds and included them in his report to the Bureau of Ethnology. For example, in 1886, the *Stevens Point Daily Journal* has a most interesting story about the discovery of

Nine-Foot Giants[54]. According to the story, on he farm of Mr. William Bush and one on the farm of Mr. Matthew Mark it was reported that many dozens of human skeletons have been exhumed from what has been called the Mark bank. Some of he skeletons were measured and the largest was found to be a little over nine feet long. At one point ten skeletons, buried in a circle, standing in an erect position and in a comparatively well-preserved condition were found. The most remarkable thing about these skeletons was the fact their teeth were in almost perfect condition.

On September 26, 1889, the *Cincinnati Courier Gazette* had another story[55] about giants. The headline was "**Gigantic Man Buried Alongside a Colossal Panther**." According to the story, this colossal man was found buried nine feet down into the mount alongside the bones of a huge panther. Below the body of the giant were the bones of a medium sized man who had around his neck a necklace containing 147 bone and shell beads. The shell beads were made from Conch and Pyrula shells that could only have come from the Atlantic Ocean.

The November 21, 1891 edition of the *Ohio Enterprise* had another unusual story about finding the grave of another giant[56].

---

[54] Powell, J.W., 12th Annual Report of the Bureau of Ethnology to the Secretary to the Smithsonian 1890-91 (Washington, D.C.: Government Printing Office, 1894)
[55] Ibid
[56] Ibid

According to this report, while digging in preparation for the World's Fair in Ohio, workers uncovered an ancient giant clad in copper. Two gentlemen by the name of Warren K. Morehead and Dr. Cresson were excavating a mound on the Hopewell Farm, a location that contained some twenty or so Indian Mounds. On this particular day they were excavating a huge mound, over 500 feet long, 200 feet wide and 28 feet high.

According to the two excavators, about 14 feet down in the center of the mound, they found the massive skeleton of a man wearing a complete set of copper armor.

The description of what was found is worth considering. The head was covered in an oval-shaped copper cap, the jaws had copper mouldings, the arms were covered in copper, while copper plates covered the chest and stomach. On each side of the head, on protruding sticks were wooden antlers ornamented with copper. In the mouth of the corpse were pearls of immense size, but the were somewhat decayed. Beside the male skeleton was found a female skeleton. It was the belief of the two that this massive figure that they had discovered was the King of the Mound Builders.

Even the Spanish Conquistadors were aware of the existence of giants in the Americas. Conquistador and Explorer Panfilo de Narvaez had conquered Jamaica and Cuba but was defeated in his attempt to conquer the natives of Northern Florida.

Finally, after losing almost half of his men to the jungle or the natives, Narvaez retreated back to Tampa Bay only to find his ships gone. With no other choice, Narvaez ordered rafts built and he and his remaining soldiers made an attempt to reach Cuba. However, they ran into a massive storm that sank most of the rafts. The last man to see Narvaez alive was Alvar Nunes Cabeza de Vaca, one of only four men to survive this ill-fated attempt to conquer Florida.

Cabeza de Vaca published the story of his adventures in the New World in 1542 and it became a major best seller in Spain. Some of his descriptions, especially of battles with giant Indians in the jungle caught the imagination of the Spanish population[57]. It was unbelievable to the average Spaniard that there were actually real live giants in the world such as he described.

Ten year later Hernando de Soto decided to conquer Florida and followed in Narvaez's footsteps. He led a fleet of nine ships into Tampa Bay with the intent of finishing what Narvaez started. As De Soto led his soldiers deeper into the jungles of Florida they met numerous tribes, each with a giant as chief. If the giant chiefs were representative of an older race than their subjects, it was clear that this older race was in decline. In less than 100 years, most of the giants were gone, but in the mounds that were left behind were skeletons attesting to the giant size these leaders

---

[57] Nunez, Alvar, *Spanish Explorers in the Southern United States: Narrative of Cabeza de Vaca* (New York: Barnes & Noble, 1959)

reached.

It should also be noted that in the reports written by Hernando De Soto's Secretary, Rodrigo Ranjel, spoke of the giant Chief Tuscaloosa[58] and his giant son. He also noted that the further west the expedition traveled the fewer giants were encountered, but more of the mysterious mounds were found[59].

As more settlers moved into Florida in the mid-1800s, they encountered numerous local legends about the giants who once inhabited the region. There were reports that some of the very early settlers saw thousands of giant skulls floating in Lake Okeechobee. It should be noted that during the drought of 2007, Lake Okeechobee's water level dropped so low that it revealed a cemetery full of ancient skeletons that were at least 7 feet in length and some that were much larger.

Of even greater interest was the fact that some of these skulls showed signs of intentional deformation like the elongated skulls found in Paracas, Peru. Some think it is very revealing that the giant chiefs of the Calusa Indians of South Florida were known as the Paracas-te, which means people of Paracas[60].

In 1925, a skull one forth larger than that of a normal

---

[58] It is interesting to note that Tuscaloosa, Alabama is named after the giant chief, Tuscaloosa defeated by de Soto.

[59] Malone, Walter, Hernando de Soto, (New York: G. P. Putnam's Sons, 1914)

[60] It should be noted that Paracas, Peru is the home to the famous Nazca Lines and many elongated skulls have been found in ancient graves nearby.

human was discovered together with bones indicating a probably height of not less than seven feet were found by workmen grading a road near the Charlotte and Lee county lines[61].

As was reported in the June 9, 1936 edition of the *New York Times*, a fisherman in Miami discovered human skeletons over eight feet long embedded in the sand of an uninhabited island of the southern tip of Florida. The discoverer brought a piece of one skull containing six teeth that was examined by E. M. Miller, zoologist at the University of Miami. Mr. Miller determined that the specimen was that of a man and was probably seven hundred years old[62].

Even officialdom does not protect an open-minded scientist from being persecuted for daring to not following accepted timelines. The first state geologist of Florida was E.H. Sellards believed that the original inhabitants of Florida was a race of giants that lived in the southeast part of the United States about 125,000 years ago.

It was this reason that he was overjoyed to be called into oversee an excavation in Vero Beach that had unearthed giant skeletons more than 12 feet in height[63]. As reported in 1917, State

---

[61] The Advertiser, "*Huge Skeleton Found in Florida,*" May 18, 1925.
[62] "*Fishermen tell of skeletons 8 feet long buried in Florida.*" The New York Times. June 9, 1936.
[63] "*Giants inhabited Florida in the Year 123,084 B.C.*" Smyrna Daily News. January 5, 1917.

Geologist E. H. Sellards and Professor Oliver P. Hay meticulously examined the skeletons and other bones found at the site. Eventually it was stated that the human bones were intermingled with those of the mastodon, saber tooth tiger and other extinct animals. Some of the skeletons were found locked in combat with some of the animal skeletons.

Of course, these discoveries did not sit well with mainstream archaeologists who insisted that the human skeletons and animals could not have existed at the same time, no matter what the physical evidence showed. From their Ivory Towers, (do not expect these leaders in the field to even think about getting their hands dirty in the field) these "scientists" made it clear that the field men were wrong and their information was bogus.

Clearly, they said, these two were wrong as the discovery of giant human remains in the Pleistocene period in North American flies in the face of established history[64]. First there were no giants, never were and could not be, let along living along side of extinct animals.

The establishment raised such a ruckus that both Sellards and Hay were forced from their positions and eventually had to leave the state to seek employment elsewhere. Once again the "accepted" theories was applied to these bones and they vanished

---

[64] Established by those in the field who had the right connections and backing by Universities.

never to be seen again. Of course, 90 years later, an amateur fossil hunter examining the Vero Beach excavation site discovered a carved mastodon bone.

In spite of the immediate attacks against this upstart who dared to question established history, three years of scientific examination resulted in this carved bit of bone being declared the oldest, most spectacular and rare work of art in the Americas[65]. Naturally, there was no mention made of the ancient giant skeletons discovered in the same strata. They were safely out of the way since they were shipped to the Smithsonian Institute and immediately vanished. Once again the Smithsonian stepped in to save the day for mainstream archaeologists.

Finally, let us cross the country to the Island of Catalina where a nine-foot tall giant skeleton was found. There are a number of Native American Middens and burial sites around the island. Prior to the advent of archaeology and its mandates that only trained scientists could excavate burial sites, there were those whose hobby was excavation of such location. One local, by the name of Ralph Glidden, claims to have discovered giant skeletons 7-8 feet tall in the Middens he excavated[66].

According to **L.A. Marzulli** in his book *Nephilim Hybrids:*

---

[65] Allen Greg, *"Florida fossil hunter gets credit for big find."* NPR, July 26, 2011.
[66] Watson, Jim, "Mysterious Island: Catalina", A Channel Catalina Publication. (2012)

Hybrids, Chimeras & Strange Demonic Creatures[67], Ralph Glidden was hired by the Heye Museum[68] to conduct primitive archaeological digs on the Channel Islands, to include Catalina. In 1919, Ralph Glidden found and photographed two nine-foot tall skeletons on Catalina. These photos were found in the Ralph Glidden collection at the Catalina Museum, but had the giant skeletons cropped out before being displayed on the wall. Someone did not want any clue as to the existence of the giant skeletons being shown.

Clearly, there are many things that science does not want the average individual to know. There are too many examples of giant skeletons found for them to be a fluke, or the result of some exotic illness or a hoax. There is no question that the history of North America is much more interesting than a few thousand primitives who cross the land bridge (which may or may not have existed) at the Bering Strait to settle here. There were clearly numerous signs of earlier advanced civilizations that have been conveniently ignored in favor of established scientific dogma. I could go on and on about discoveries that have been suppressed but this work is not meant to be a tome, but rather an over view of things that mainstream science does not want us to know about.

---

[67] Marzulli, L.A., Nephilim Hybrids: Hybrids, Chimeras & Strange Demonic Creatures, Amazon Kindle, 2016.
[68] The Heye Museum was eventually taken over by the Smithsonian Institute.

It is also very interesting to know that our forces in Afghanistan have had contact with red haired giants who are eager for battle. There is a story told to me by a military pilot I met that one of his friends had been called upon to fly a dead 15 foot tall giant from a location in a remote valley to a base and then, once it was placed in a crate to an airfield for a flight to somewhere classified. Imagine my surprise when I saw the same or a similar story repeated in Marzulli's book.

That being said let us now turn our attention to animals that can't possibly exist.

CHAPTER SEVEN

STRANGE CREATURES FROM TIME AND SPACE

In spite of the assurance from science that many of the exotic creatures that we read about are just hoaxes or misidentification of normal creatures, there are still a number of questions that have to be answered. Let's see if we can determine what some of the questions might be.

REAL DRAGONS AND OTHER CREATURES

The first question in this exploration of the strange and the unusual is whether or not dragons are real or just figments of our imagination or the inhabitants of a fairy tail. The first place to look for confirmation would be historical records. Naturally, the first place that most people would look to would be the Holy Bible, probably the most familiar book to many people and still the best selling book of all time.

In spite of our familiarity with this book and its teachings (if you ever went to Sunday School it was drilled into you) most are not aware that the idea of real dragons is actually consistent with the Bible. In the Book of Genesis it is written that on Day 5 of Creation, God created great "sea creatures[69]" and flying creatures. This would naturally have included such things as the Pliosaurs

---

[69] The Hebrew word is tanninim.

and Pterodactyls. Assuming that the Book of Genesis has any validity as to God creating the world in 7 days, there is no doubt that Man co-existed with these great creatures, or the Thunder Lizards as many call them.

Multiple times in Scripture the Hebrew word tannin has been used. This little known word is defined by the *Enhanced Brown-Driver-Briggs Hebrew and English Lexicon* as "serpent, dragon, sea monster." Whatever it may be referring to, there is no doubt that it is referring to a reptile.

Now I am sure at this point, forgetting that Bible is actually a history book of great historic value, there are a number of people who are ready to put this book down as a bunch of religious hooey. Well, for you folks, lets look at other sources of information regarding the existence of dragons.

We can start at the Maritime Aquarium at Norwalk in the town of Norwalk, Connecticut. One of the exhibits is of the melanistic (black) Asian water monitor lizard that grows to six feet long and weighs approximately 60 pounds as an adult. Something the size of this very rare creature could certainly qualify for the name of dragon.

Of course, let's not forget about the Komodo Dragon, which can top the scales at 150 pounds. Compare this with the saltwater crocodile that can grow to 20 feet in length and weigh as much as 2,000 pounds. While this may seem huge, let us not forget the largest of the dinosaurs, the Titanosaurs, which exceeded 130 feet in length and weighed as much as 90 etic tons.

On UTUBE.com there are numerous videos of alleged dragons or at least some flying creatures that are totally bizarre and unlike anything anyone has ever seen. Make no mistake, there are many unexplained creatures inhabiting our planet.

In addition to the better known flying reptiles, there have also been numerous other creatures found that are never publically discussed by our "betters." One of these creatures was found in Mexico as discussed by L.A. Marzulli in his book *Nephilim Hybrids: Hybrids, Chimeras & Strange Demonic Creatures*[70].

L.A. Marzulli[71] and Richard Shaw flew to Mexico to interview Jaime Maussan[72] whom they described as one of the leading UFO experts in the world. Jaime Maussan was the host of a weekly television show about UFOs and related topics.

As discussed in his book, Jaime Maussan showed him two dead creatures that stood almost a foot tall and had wings that appeared to be naturally occurring. For all practical purposes these

---

[70] Marzulli, L.A., Nephilim Hybrids: Hybrids, Chimeras & Strange Demonic Creatures, Amazon Kindle, 2016.
[71] L. A. Marzulli is the author of the best selling Nephilim Trilogy, Politics, Prophecy & the Supernatural and the Alien Interviews. He has appeared on hundreds of radio and television programs and is a sought after conference speaker.
[72] José Jaime Maussan Flota (born May 31, 1953) is a **Mexican journalist**, television personality and **ufologist**.

things looked like tiny humans at least their appearance was that of a tiny humanoid, with two hands and two feet.

As discussed in his book, L.A. Marzulli talked to those who both X-rayed as well as conducted DNA testing on their two creatures. The DNA tests were conducted by Ricardo Rangel, Ph.D. Dr. Rangel reported that his tests showed that most of the DNA found in the creatures pointed to a human origin, but some of the DNA was unknown to science[73].

In a later discussion, Jaime Maussan reported that the DNA testing he had performed on the mysterious creatures showed that the mitochondrial DNA was clearly human, but the nuclear DNA was unknown. Since the creatures in question were found in Mexico, if they are being created in a lab, it is probably in Mexico, though it may be funded by U.S. backers who use the difference in laws to circumvent the laws here prohibiting such experimentation.

Less the reader thinks this is the wildest fantasy, it has been reported that labs in the United Kingdom had created chimeras[74],

---

[73] Marzulli, L.A., <u>Nephilim Hybrids: Hybrids, Chimeras & Strange Demonic Creatures</u>, Amazon Kindle, 2016.

[74] A genetic chimerism or chimera (also spelled chimaera) is a single organism composed of cells from different zygotes. This can result in male and female organs, two blood types, or subtle variations in form. Animal chimeras are produced by the merger of multiple fertilized eggs. In plant chimeras, however, the distinct types of tissue may originate from the same zygote, and the difference is often due to mutation during ordinary cell division. Normally, genetic chimerism is not visible on casual inspection; however, it has been detected in the course of proving parentage. Another way that chimerism can occur in animals is by organ

but then destroyed them. However, when has a scientist ever just abandoned a field of study where he or she had achieved success?

It should also be noted that X-Rays taken of these creatures showed the presence of implants similar to the implants found in humans who have come in contact with UFOs. If they are being bred, so to speak, perhaps these implants allow tracking of the creatures in the event of their escape.

OTHER ODD CREATURES

From Mexico let us go to St. Louis, Missouri and a story from the St. Louis *Globe-Democrat* dated January 17, 1885. According to the reporter, some hunters in Vincennes, Indiana were startled to encounter what they called a horrible looking creature. They described this creature as having a head and face resembling a dark-skinned human with a very large moth full of sharp, fan-like teeth. Its neck was two or three feet long and covered with short red colored hair; its body was five or six feet in length and was covered with scales that looked bright like those of a sun-fish; its tail was three or four feet long and curved up over its back; its legs were short and the feet were webbed and the toes had

---

transplantation, giving one individual tissues that developed from two genomes. For example, a bone marrow transplant can change someone's blood type.

long claws [75]. When first seen, the creatures had been rapidly devouring a hog, which it held easily in its hands.

Seeing as there were several hunters and only one of the creatures, the heroes of this story decided to capture the creature. In the ensuing struggle, they discovered that the creature was unusually powerful for its size and that there were not enough hunters to overpower the creature. Needless to say, it escaped.

In 1937, a horrified fisherman watched what he described as a green-colored, scaly humanoid emerge from a lake in Saginaw, Michigan where he had been peacefully fishing. The creature stood motionless on the shore in the shadow of a tree until it spotted the fisherman. Realizing it was not along the creature dove back into the lake and the fisherman made an equally rapid departure in the other direction.

In 1944, a fisherman in Alaska by the name of Frank Read reported that he had discovered a human-like creature attacking one of his fish traps. According to Mr. Read, the creature had a human head, narrow shoulders, long, sharp claws and a long tail. When it realized that it was being watched, the creature rapidly dove into the water and vanished and Mr. Read rapidly went in the other direction [76].

---

[75] Nunnelly, Barton M., The Inhumanoids: Real Life Encounters With Beings that Can't Exist, Triangulum Publishing, 2017.
[76] Ibid and also Alaska Life Magazine

Evidence would seem to indicate that these scaly creatures might have been some of the mysterious merfolk of legend. There have been stories about these creatures going back eons; in fact almost every culture has stories of creatures that live beneath the sea. Making the story even more interesting, the early Babylonians passed down stories form the ancient Sumerian culture that claimed that it was a creature from the sea that taught them everything they knew about mathematics, writing, and agriculture. This entity, looked at as a god was called Oannes.

A number of cultures in the Middle East had gods who resembled Oannes. The gods of the ancient Egyptians bore a remarkable resemblance to the Babylonian gods. The only difference was that their aquatic god had muscular legs with webbed feet beneath their fishy tails.

The ancient Sumerians called these creatures *Abgal*, while the Nordic legends called them *Nykkjen*. The Maori referred to these ancient creatures as the *Horomatangi*, though they believed that these creatures were evil cannibals who had a liking for human flesh. The Japanese were familiar with the Kappa, which was said to have the body of a tortoise, an ape-like head, scaly limbs with webbed hands and feet and an odor of fish.

The Japanese were also aware of the *Samebito* or shark men, said to be fearsome black and green skinned aquatic humanoids with glowing eyes. The Zulus of South Africa were (and probably still are) terrified of the *Mbulus*, frightening lizard men who are humanoid in shape with scaly skin, sharp teeth, claws and a long tail.

These aquatic bringers of knowledge lost their divine status with the advent of Christianity and took on the trappings of devils since the early fanatical followers of Jesus looked at anything strange as being of the devil. Though today, the mention of mermaid will usually bring a mental picture of a beautiful woman with a fish tail to mind.

It should be noted that there is a large body of stories regarding merfolk who have allegedly been captured and who instinctively knew to worship the cross. How many of these stories were told to elevate the power of the Cross and how many were true is anyone's guess. However, stories such as these are found in almost very culture in the world.

THE SERPENT MEN

Numerous volumes have been written about the serpent people which have also been referred to in UFO lore as Reptilians. Many researchers believe that these creatures exited prior to the advent of the human race and others believe that they may be an inevitable evolution of the dinosaurs. Naturally, there are those who believe that these creatures are inherently evil and want to destroy mankind.

There is a believe to be found among Christian fundamentalists that there was a race of serpent men that existed at the time of the Garden of Eden and it was one of these creatures that was influenced by Lucifer to seduce Eve and cause her to break the laws of God.

Of course, there is another story that Adam's first wife was one of the Serpent People named Lilith. She is supposed to have seduced Eve out of revenge for being spurned by Adam. Whatever may be the truth regarding the Serpent People, there is no question that they are still making appearances and interacting with humans. Now the question becomes are these the same Serpent People said to live beneath Los Angles, California. Consider the following news report.

LIZARD PEOPLE'S CATACOMB CITY HUNTED
Engineer Sinks Shaft Under Fort Moore Hill to Find Maze of Tunnels and Priceless Treasures of Legendary Inhabitants
LA Times, 29 Jan 1934
By Jean Bosquet

Busy Los Angeles, although little realizing it in the hustle and bustle of modern existence, stands above a lost city of catacombs filled with incalculable treasure and imperishable records of a race of humans further advanced intellectually and scientifically than even the highest type of present day peoples, in the belief of G. Warren Shufelt, geophysical engineer now engaged in an attempt to wrest from the lost city deep in the earth below

Fort Moore Hill the secrets of the Lizard People of legendary fame in the medicine lodges of the American Indian.

So firmly does Shufelt and a little staff of assistants believe that a maze of catacombs and priceless golden tablets are to be found beneath downtown Los Angeles that the engineer and his aides have already driven a shaft 250 feet into the ground, the mouth of the shaft being on the old Banning property on North Hill street overlooking Sunset Boulevard, Spring street and North Broadway.

LEGEND SUPPLIES CLEW

Shufelt learned of the legend of the Lizard People after his radio X-ray had led him hither and yon, over an area extending from the Public Library on West Fifth Street to the Southwest Museum, on Museum Drive, at the foot of Mt. Washington.

"I knew I was over a pattern of tunnels," the engineer explained yesterday, "and I had mapped out the course of the tunnels, the position of large rooms scattered along the tunnel route, as well as the position of deposits of gold, but I couldn't understand the meaning of it."

FIRE DESTROYS ALL

According to the legend as imparted to Shufelt by Macklin, the radio X-ray has revealed the location of one of three lost cities on the Pacific Coast, the local one having been dug by the Lizard People after the "great catastrophe" which occurred about 5000 years ago. This legendary catastrophe was in the form of a huge tongue of fire that "came out of the Southwest, destroying all life in its path," the path being "several hundred miles wide." The city underground was dug as a means of escaping future fires.

The lost city, dug with powerful chemicals by the Lizard People instead of pick and shovel, was drained into the ocean, where its tunnels began, according to the legend. The tide passing daily in and out of the lower tunnel portals and forcing air into the upper tunnels, provided ventilation and "cleansed and sanitized the lower tunnels," the legend states.

Large rooms in the domes of the hills above the city of labyrinths housed 1000 families "in the manner of tall buildings" and imperishable food supplies of the herb variety were stored in the catacombs to provide sustenance for the lizard folk for great lengths of time as the next fire swept over the earth.

CITY LAID OUT LIKE LIZARD

The Lizard People, the legend has it, regarded the lizard as the symbol of long life. Their city is laid out like a lizard, according to the legend, its tail to the southwest, far below Fifth and Hope streets, its head to the northeast, at Lookout and Marda streets. The city's key room is situated directly under South Broadway, near Second Street, according to Shufelt and the legend.

This key room is the directory to all parts of the city and to all record tablets, the legend states. All records were kept on gold tablets, four feet long and fourteen inches wide. On these tablets of gold, gold having been the symbol of life to the legendary Lizard People, will be found the recorded history of the Mayans on one particular tablet, the southwest corner of which will be missing, is to be found the "record of the origin of the human race."

TABLETS PHOTOGRAPHED

Shufelt stated he has taken "X-ray pictures" of thirty-seven such tablets, three of which have their southwest corners cut off.

"My radio X-ray pictures of tunnels and rooms, which are sub-surface voids, and of gold pictures with perfect corners, sides and ends, are scientific proof of their existence," Shufelt said. "However, the legendary story must remain speculative until unearthed by excavation."

The Lizard People according to Macklin were of a much higher type intellectually than modern human beings. The intellectual accomplishments of their 9-year-old children were the equal of those of present day college graduates, he said. So greatly advanced scientifically were these people that, in addition to perfecting a chemical solution by which they bored underground without removing earth and rock, they also developed a cement far stronger and better than any in use in modern times with which they lined their tunnels and rooms.

HILLS ENCLOSE CITY

Macklin said legendary advice to American Indians was to seek the lost city in an area within a chain of hills forming "the frog of a horse's hoof." The contour of hills surrounding this region forms such a design, substantiating Shufelt's findings, he said.

Shufelt's radio device consists chiefly of a cylindrical glass case inside of which a plummet attached to a copper wire held by the engineer sways continually, pointing, he asserts, toward minerals or tunnels below the surface of the ground, and then revolves when over the mineral or swings in prolongation of the tunnel when above the excavation.

He has used the instrument extensively in mining fields, he said.

DID STRANGE PEOPLE LIVE UNDER SITE OF LOS ANGELES 5000 YEARS AGO?

An amazing labyrinth of underground passages and caverns hundreds of feet below the surface of Fort Moore Hill is revealed in maps – all rights to which have been reserved – prepared by G. Warren Shufelt, local mining engineer, who explains his topographical endeavors as being based on results obtained from a radio X-ray perfected by him. In this elaborate system of tunnels and rooms, according to a legend furnished Shufelt by an Indian authority, a tribe of human beings called the Lizard People, lived,

5000 years ago.

The network of tunnels formed what Indians call the lost Lizard City, according to Shufelt and the legend. Gold tablets on which are written the origin of the human race and other priceless documents are to be found in the tunnels, according to the legend. Shufelt declares his radio X-ray has located the gold. The engineer has dug a shaft 250 feet deep on North Hill Street, overlooking North Broadway, Sunset and Spring streets, and intends to dig to 1000 feet in an effort to strike the lost city[77].

---

[77] Copyright ©: Stephanie Relfe 2014 – 3000
This article, or parts of this article may be copied as long as no alterations are made, you mention and link to www.Metatech.org or www.Relfe.com.

ANCIENT SECRETS /121

pg. A1 Jan 29, 1934 *Los Angeles Times*

LIZARD PEOLPE'S CATACOMB CITY HUN

Engineer Sinks Shaft Under Fort Moore Hill to Find Maze of Tunn Priceless Treasures of Legendary Inhabitants

BY JEAN BOSQUET

Busy Los Angeles, although little realizing it in the hustle and bustle of modern existence, stand lost city of catacombs filled with incalculable treasure and imperishable records of a race of humans f vanced intellectually and scientifically than even the highest type of present day peoples, in the be Warren Shufelt, geophysical mining engineer now engaged in an attempt to wrest from the lost in the earth below Fort Moore Hill the secrets of the Lizard People of legendary fame in the mem of the American Indian.

So firmly does Shufelt and a little staff of assistants believe that a maze of catacombs and priceless golden tablets are to be found beneath downtown Los Angeles that the engineer and his aides have already driven a shaft 250 feet into the ground, the mouth of the shaft being on the old Banning property on North Hill street overlooking Sunset Boulevard, Spring street and North Broadway.

And so convinced is the engineer of the infallibility of a radio X-ray perfected by him for detecting the presence of minerals and tunnels below the surface of the ground, an apparatus with which he says he has traced a pattern of catacombs and vaults forming the lost city, that he plans to continue sending his shaft downward until he has reached a depth of 1000 feet before discontinuing operations.

LEGEND SUPPLIES CLEW

Shufelt learned of the legend of the Lizard People after his radio X-ray had led him hither and yon, over an area extending from the Public Library on West Fifth street to the Southwest Museum, on Museum Drive, at the foot of Mt. Washington.

"I knew I was over a pattern of tunnels," the engineer explained yesterday, "and I had mapped out the course of the tunnels, the position of large rooms scattered along the tunnel route, as well as the position of deposits of gold, but I couldn't understand the meaning of it."

Then Shufelt was taken to Little Chief Greenleaf of the medicine lodge of the Hopi Indians in Arizona, whose English name is L. Macklin. The Indian provided the engineer with a legend which, according to both men, dovetails exactly with what Shufelt says he has found.

FIRE DESTROYS ALL

According to the legend as imparted to Shufelt by Macklin, the radio X-ray has revealed the location of one of three lost cities on the Pacific Coast, the local one having been dug by the Lizard People after the "great e which occurred about ago. This legendary catas in the form of a huge fire which "came out of west, destroying all life in the path being "several miles wide." The city w was dug as a means o future fires.

The lost city, dug wit chemicals by the Lizard stead of pick and sh drained into the ocean, tunnels began, accordi legend. The tide passin and out of the lower t tals and forcing air into tunnels, provided ventil "cleansed and sanitized tunnels," the legend stat

Large rooms in the do hills above the city of housed 1000 families "in ner of tall buildings" and able food supplies of riety were stored in the to provide sustenance for folk for great lengths the next fire swept earth.

DID STRANGE PEOPLE LIVE UNDER SITE O

An amazing labyrinth of underground passages and caverns hundreds of feet below the sur served—prepared by G. Warren Shufelt, local mining engineer, who explains his topographical him. In this elaborate system of tunnels and rooms, according to a legend furnished Shufelt by years ago. The network of tunnels formed what Indians call the lost Lizard City, according to human race and other priceless documents are to be found in the tunnels, according to the legend a shaft 250 feet deep on North Hill street, overlooking North Broadway, Sunset and Spring stre hand corner inset is Times Staff Artist Ewing's conception of the Lizard People at work. Lowe their deep excavation. Lower left inset shows Shufelt operating his radio X-ray device.

If there were such a civilization living underground, it would explain many legends of the old west. There have long been stories of lizard people living in caves in the west. Certainly, the proven fact that a race of giants co-existed (and may still do so) with the human race confirms that our science does not know everything about who inhabits this mud ball that we call earth.

Across this country have come reports of humanoid like frogs and other aquatic creatures. Example of this would be the Ohio frogman that was seen for the first time at Branch Hill, Ohio in March of 1955. This fist siting was by a businessman who actually saw three of these creatures kneeling beside the road. He described them as being about 3 feet tall with long slender arms; frog faces with normal appearing human eyes without eyebrows. He also stated that the creatures were wearing gray colored tight fitting clothing and their exposed skin was gray.

The next reported sighting was by a policeman in the early 1970s in Loveland, Ohio who saw several creatures similar in appearance. The question now becomes, what other creatures can be found in the night?

CHAPTER EIGHT

HUMANITY'S INHUMAN GUIDES

In our modern civilization we believe that there are few secrets still left to be discovered. In actuality, nothing could be further from the truth; there are many secrets still to be uncovered. Let us look at some of these secrets that are right in front of our noses.

In the nursery rhymes that we all are told as kids, there are numerous stories of otherworldly creatures that come to either help or hinder characters in these stories. It makes for some of the most fascinating parts of these stories. What few are aware of is that there really are strange creatures that have come to help or hinder mankind and some are even stranger than those from our fantasies. This is a case of truth being stranger than fiction.

Naturally no discussion of otherworldly creatures would be complete without a reference to Oannes, the half man, half fish who the ancient Sumerians claimed came from the depths of the ocean to teach humanity the basics of civilization. It is interesting to note that Oannes never ate any of the food offered to him and returned to the depths each evening. Now, let's look at some of the other unusual entities that have been encountered by unsuspecting humans. In the rest of this chapter, we will deal with visitations that affected the course of human history.

JOAN OF ARC

Let us first start with the mysterious voices heard by Joan of Arc. Though a peasant girl, Joan followed her voices to become the leader of the French Army and come very close to freeing her country from he English. It is clear that if she had not been betrayed by her own people and handed over to the English as a witch, she would have succeeded[78]. Was she a military genius as described by some or guided by God as was said by others, or perhaps even a witch as her detractors claimed. This has never been answered.

History tells us that Joan of Arc was burned at the stake as a witch; however, this may not be what actually happened. It seems that English soldiers surrounded the location where she was to have been burned and all others were kept at a distance, too far to actually confirm the identity of the person tied to the stake. Several years later, a woman of the right age appeared in France claiming to be Joan. Her own family accepted her as Joan and she

---

[78] Nunnelly, Barton, *The Inhumanoids: Real Encounters With Beings that Can't Exist*, Triangle Publishing, 2017, Kindle Edition.

reported her death had been faked. So the question becomes what is the truth.

GEORGE WASHINGTON

It was reported that in the winter of 1777, when the colonists were at their lowest point in the war against the British, at Valley Forge, George Washington had a strange visitor. According to what Washington is said to have reported to his friend Anthony Sherman, this visitor was a red skinned figure with long hair wearing a dark robe[79].

According to what Washington said to his friend Anthony Sherman, this entity showed him a vision of the birth, progress and destiny of the new country they were in the process of trying to establish. It was reported that this vision gave Washington the courage to continue the struggle against the most powerful army in the world.

It would seem that the mysterious creatures that seem to inhabit our world with us had an interest in politics and wanted the United States to be established as a separate country.

NAPOLEON BONAPARTE

Another name in history that is said to have been guided by these mysterious entities was Napoleon Bonaparte. This man, who eventually became the Emperor of France has been described as

---

[79] Some have said the figure that appeared to Georgia Washington was female, others that it was a male. It is interesting to note that in the Bible, most Angeles were described as male.

simply lucky by some or a military genius by others. There is little question that he appeared to outthink his opponents and his armies outfought his enemies. Then it all came crashing down seemingly over night. What was the truth about this man's career?

Based on reports from his own staff, there is little doubt that a red skinned entity came to visit Napoleon from time to time. It is believed by many that the entity first visited the "Little Corporal" during his campaign in Egypt[80].

According to the story, one evening after the bloody "Battle of the Pyramids" Napoleon was pouring over his maps when this figure suddenly appeared in his bedchamber. When Napoleon demanded to know the identity of the entity, he (because it was clearly a male) replied that he had given advice and counsel to the rulers of France for many years and come to warn Napoleon of certain mistakes he had made in his plans.

The entity is said to have admonished Napoleon for his ambition and his lust for power. Napoleon, based upon what is known about him would probably have replied he only did what was best for France.

The red-hued visitor told Napoleon that his orders to the French fleet had not been carried out and that his Egyptian campaign would be a failure. He also warned Napoleon that he

---

[80] Nunnelly, Barton, *The Inhumanoids: Real Encounters With Beings that Can't Exist*, Triangle Publishing, 2017, Kindle Edition.

would return to France to find her surrounded by her enemies. He was warned that there would be mobs in the street confronting him when he returned home. Startled, Napoleon found that everything the man had said to him came to pass.

It has been said that the red skinned figure made three visits to Napoleon. The second visit took place in 1809 after the Battle of Wagram. The third visit was made on the morning of January 1, 1814 shortly before Napoleon was forced to abdicate as Emperor of France.

It was on this third visit that the mysterious visitor was seen face to face by a witness, none other than the Counselor of State. Napoleon had left orders not to be disturbed, so the mysterious red skinned figure appeared to the Counselor of State demanding to see Napoleon on maters of great importance. The Counselor or State refused the visitor admittance, but he did notify Napoleon of the individual's request. To everyone's shock, Napoleon granted him immediate entrance to his bedchamber.

It was reported that Napoleon literally begged this individual for more time to complete his plans. The entity is reported to have stated that he was neither deity nor prophet, but merely a messenger. He gave Napoleon three months to achieve a general peace or it would all be over for him.

In an effort to gain more time, Napoleon set out on a new eastern campaign that failed. On April 1, 1814, the French Senate called for Napoleon's abdication. Once again, the prediction of the mysterious red skinned entity was shown to be correct.

KING CHARLES XII

King Charles XII was the King of Sweden and a brilliant military leader. In fact, he demonstrated such military brilliance that he was referred to by many as the Alexander of the North. Some of those close to him reported that he allegedly sought council from a figure referred to by most as a "Little Gray Man". The skin of the "Little Gray Man" was described as reddish or ruddy.

According to the stories of those closest to him King Charles XII had been given a magic ring by the "Little Gray Man". It was said the ring would not vanish until the day of the King's death.

The military victories achieved by the Alexander of the North were legendary. He cut a broad swath across Europe, Russia and Turkey achieving victories against impossible odds. However, just as happened to Napoleon, he refused to see peace as his red skinned advisor insisted.

So it was that in 1718 during one of his many battle, at the siege of Fredrikshald, one of his men noticed that the ring was no long on his finger. As soon as it was brought to his attention, King Charles XII fell from his horse. He had been hit in the head and died instantly. The ring was never found.

ADOLF HITLER

Adolf Hitler is another who has been described both as a lunatic and a military genius. Surely, he held human life in little regard. There are also numerous books that discuss the use of Black Magic as a weapon by the Nazi inner circle and there is little doubt that Himmler was guided by dreams of ancient glory.

However, the question we must answer is whether or not mysterious entities appeared to or guided any of the Nazi hierarchy. The answer must be answered in the affirmative; there is little question that Hitler was visited in his quarters by entities unseen by even his guards.

On more than one occasion, he made the statement to one of his associates that he had seen the "new man". He further went on to state *"He is intrepid and cruel. I was afraid of him."*

There are also a number of military leaders from the era that the Adolf Hitler that began World War II was a military genius. His plans almost always came to fruition resulting in Germany out maneuvering his opponents in a number of bloodless victories. It was only later in the war that his genius seemed to desert him. Some say that he was actually assassinated early in the war and replaced with a double[81] that was clearly not a military genius. Others believe that he was receiving guidance from one of

---

[81] It was well know that Hitler had several doubles that could easily have fooled those who did not know him well.

the mysterious new men he talked about. Apparently, the new men abandoned him. Or perhaps the truth was a combination of the two possibilities. At this late date, we will probably never know.

OLIVER CROMWELL

The name Oliver Cromwell is very well known in English history. Some honor his name and others vilify it. Oliver Cromwell [82] was an English military and political leader and later Lord Protector of the Commonwealth of England, Scotland, and Ireland. He was also said to be one of those who benefited fro the guidance from the unknown.

Cromwell was born into the middle gentry, albeit to a family descended from the sister of King Henry VIII's minister Thomas Cromwell. Little is known of the first 40 years of his life as only four of his personal letters survive alongside a summary of a speech he delivered in 1628.

He became an Independent Puritan after undergoing a religious conversion in the 1630s, taking a generally tolerant view towards the many Protestant sects of his period. He was an intensely religious man, a self-styled Puritan Moses, and he fervently believed that God was guiding his victories. He was elected Member of Parliament for Huntingdon in 1628 and for Cambridge in what was called the Short (1640) and Long (1640–1649) parliaments.

---

[82] (25 April 1599 – 3 September 1658)

He entered the English Civil War on the side of the "Roundheads" or Parliamentarians. Nicknamed "Old Ironsides", he demonstrated his ability as a commander and was quickly promoted from leading a single cavalry troop to being one of the principal commanders of the New Model Army, playing an important role in the defeat of the royalist forces.

Cromwell was one of the signatories of King Charles I's death warrant in 1649, and he dominated the short-lived Commonwealth of England as a member of the Rump Parliament (1649–1653). He was selected to take command of the English campaign in Ireland in 1649–1650. Cromwell's forces defeated the Confederate and Royalist coalition in Ireland and occupied the country, bringing to an end the Irish Confederate Wars. During this period, a series of Penal Laws were passed against Roman Catholics (a significant minority in England and Scotland but the vast majority in Ireland), and a substantial amount of their land was confiscated. Cromwell also led a campaign against the Scottish army between 1650 and 1651.

On 20 April 1653, he dismissed the Rump Parliament by force, setting up a short-lived nominated assembly known as Barebone's Parliament, before being invited by his fellow leaders to rule as Lord Protector of England (which included Wales at the time), Scotland and Ireland from 16 December 1653.[3] As a ruler, he executed an aggressive and effective foreign policy. He died from natural causes in 1658 and was buried in Westminster Abbey. The Royalists returned to power in 1660, and they had his corpse dug up, hung in chains, and beheaded.

In the English Civil War that led to his assumption of power, Parliamentarians, loyal to <u>Oliver Cromwell</u>, were doing battle around the country to overthrow Royalist forces. Having already executed King Charles I in 1649, Cromwell had recently won victory at the Battle of Dunbar, capturing Edinburgh.

The Scottish wanted to see King Charles I's son, also called Charles, put on the throne, and Cromwell's forces defeated. With Scottish allies, Charles was made King of Scotland. Cromwell's men had brutally slain men, women, and children north of the English border, and the consensus was that he had to be stopped at all costs. Charles II and his forces subsequently made an attempt to invade England and capture London whilst Cromwell was still engaged in Scotland.

The year was 1651, and they had got as far as the city of Worcester. Followed by Cromwell and his men, the march to London had been abruptly halted, with the Parliamentarian army making ready to strike.

In order to further increase their defenses the Royalists were given the order to blow up four key bridges that gave access to Worcester. This bought the King's forces some respite, yet Cromwell was not discouraged, and sent one of his Generals, John

Lambert, south to Upton-upon-Severn. Seizing the damaged bridge with his unit of Dragoons, Lambert had it rebuilt, and soon the Parliamentarian forces had Worcester surrounded.

By this point, Cromwell had around 31,000 men. The city of Worcester was ringed around the south and east, and to the north. All that could be done was to hold themselves in a siege and hope that reinforcements or some miracle would arrive. Surely God himself was on the side of the true King and his loyalists.

Cromwell had chosen to site his camps around Perry Wood and Red Hill, which gave him cannon range over the city. Fond of his large artillery, he used a favored method of blasting structures to smithereens. Evidence of this destructive method can still be seen in Britain and Ireland, where his troops had been ordered to blow up castles and other stately homes so that they could not be re-claimed for use by the enemy.

The Parliamentarians seemingly took their time. It was not until a council of war took place, that the attack to seize Worcester really took momentum. Cromwell's forces were split in half to cut off the escape from the city, and it is at this point in history that the tale takes a turn for the supernatural.

It is said that on the morning of September 3rd, a visitor arrived at Cromwell's camp in Perry Wood. Part of the vast and ancient Feckenham Forest, the area was already steeped in legends and superstition, so it is not surprising that such an event should take place.

Not wanting to go to this meeting with the visitor alone, it was said that Cromwell decided that he take Colonel Lindsay, first Captain of Oliver Cromwell's own regiment with him. In later reports, Colonel Lindsay describes how he was taken with Cromwell himself to the Feckenham Forest. Sensing something wrong, Lindsay claims he refused to dismount and follow Cromwell into the woods.

Cromwell finally agreed but told Lindsay to watch closely everything that happened. According to Lindsay, Cromwell walked bravely to the edge of the woods where he met 'a grave elderly man wearing a dark robe who carried a roll of parchment in his hand'. Lindsay reported that the mere sight of this man filled Lindsay with an uncontrollable horror and trembling, as he realized who this visitor really was. He claimed that the old man was the Devil himself.

According to Lindsay he heard the old one promise Cromwell that he would have his will then, and in all things else for seven years', at which date it would be his – the devil's – turn to have complete mastery over Cromwell's soul and body."

Cromwell objected stating loudly that he had ben promised 10 years with the possibility of twenty years. According to the tale, Cromwell had argued with the Devil over this short span, expecting twenty-one years. After much bickering, Lindsay said that Cromwell finally agreed to the seven years. As he left the woods to rejoin the Colonel, Lindsay reported that Cromwell cried out joyously to the Colonel, "Now Lindsay, the Battle is our own, I long to be engaged."

Reportedly, completely unnerved by what he had seen, Colonel Lindsay deserted, galloping away at first charge, lest he be damned to the Devil along with his General, whilst Cromwell fought in the final battle with wanton confidence, and leading his men himself.

The large Parliamentarian army, closed in on the city and in a last desperate attempt of redemption, Charles II led a personal sally towards the east. Working their way uphill into Perry Wood, they were met with pike and gun, and were subsequently routed and driven back to Worcester.

Fleeing back into the city, Cromwell's forces closed in on the Royalists, and the streets ran red with blood. Worcester city was littered with the bodies of men and horse, blocking passage through the streets in heaps. Two thousand men were slain at a cost of two hundred of Cromwell's. Around nine thousand prisoners were taken, with the terrified Royalists surrendering to their enemies.

Worcester had fallen. The last major Scottish Royalist army had been destroyed, with those that survived being sent off to the colonies to serve as little more than slaves as indentured laborers. Charles II fled to France and the Netherlands.

So did Cromwell's rule extend the twenty or so years he had demanded? He did indeed win the English Civil War, yet he died on September 3rd, 1658, exactly seven years after his pact with the Devil in Perry Woods. Was this the devil that had made the bargain with Cromwell or one of the mysterious guides that have popped up in history from time to time?

Based on the stories above, it would probably be wise to wonder how many leaders of history were guided from the shadows by unknown entities. It would explain many of history's mysteries to discover that these stories have a basis in truth.

CHAPTER NINE
OTHER MYSTERIOUS CREATURES

Based on the many reports that we have reviewed in preparation for this book, there is no doubt that there is an entire world of strange creatures of which most of us have no inkling. These stories come from almost every state and every era of history. In this chapter, we will review a few of the better-known reports of strange creatures from time and space.

MOTHMAN

One of the best known of these mysterious denizens of the dark is probably the creature referred to as Mothman. Most relatively recent stories about Mothman seem to come from the state of West Virginia. In West Virginia folklore, the Mothman is a legendary creature reportedly seen in the Point Pleasant area from November 12, 1966, to December 15, 1967.

The first newspaper report was published in the Point Pleasant Register dated November 16, 1966, titled "*Couples See*

Man-Sized Bird ... Creature ... Something"[83]. The national press soon picked up the reports and helped spread the story across the country.

The creature known as Mothman was introduced to a wider audience by author Gray Barker in 1970[84][85] and later popularized by the legendary John Keel in his 1975 book The Mothman Prophecies, claiming that there were supernatural events related to the sightings, and a connection to the collapse of the Silver Bridge.

The Mothman is the subject of regional folklore and popular culture. The 2002 film The Mothman Prophecies, starring Richard Gere, was based on Keel's book[86]. An annual festival in Point Pleasant is devoted to the Mothman legend.

On November 12, 1966, five men who were digging a grave at a cemetery near Clendenin, West Virginia, claimed to see a man-like figure fly low from the trees over their heads.[5] This is

---

[83] "Couples See Man-Sized Bird...Creature...Something". Point Pleasant Register Point Pleasant, WV Wednesday, November 16, 1966. WestVA.Net, Mark Turner.

[84] *Skeptical Inquirer*, Volume 33 (Pennsylvania State University, Committee for the Scientific Investigation of Claims of the Paranormal., 2009).

[85] **Barker,** Gray, *The Silver Bridge* (Saucerian Books, 1970). Reprinted in 2008 entitled *The Silver Bridge: The Classic Mothman Tale* (BookSurge Publishing). ISBN 1-4392-0427-6

[86] Keel, John A. *The Mothman Prophecies* (2007). ISBN 0-7653-4197-2 (Originally published in 1975 by Saturday Review Press)

incident is often identified as the first known sighting of what later became known as the Mothman[87].

Shortly thereafter, on November 15, 1966, two young couples from Point Pleasant, Roger and Linda Scarberry and Steve and Mary Mallette, told police they saw a large black creature whose eyes "glowed red" when the car headlights picked it up. They described it as a "large flying man with ten-foot wings", following their car while they were driving in an area outside of town known as "the TNT area", the site of a former World War II munitions plant.[88]

- During the next few days, other people reported similar sightings. Two volunteer firemen who sighted it said it was a "large bird with red eyes".
- Mason County Sheriff George Johnson commented that he believed the sightings were due to an unusually large heron he termed a "shitepoke".
- Contractor Newell Partridge told Johnson that when he aimed a flashlight at a creature in a nearby field its eyes glowed "like bicycle reflectors", and blamed buzzing noises

---

[87] "First sighting of the Mothman". Wvcommerce.org. 1966-11-12.
[88] Nickell, Joe (April 2004). _The Mystery Chronicles: More Real-Life X-Files_. University Press of Kentucky. ISBN 978-0-8131-2318-9. Retrieved 21 August 2011.

from his television set and the disappearance of his German Shepherd dog on the creature.[8]

- Wildlife biologist Dr. Robert L. Smith at West Virginia University told reporters that descriptions and sightings all fit the sandhill crane, a large American crane almost as high as a man with a seven-foot wingspan featuring circles of reddish coloring around the eyes, and that the bird may have wandered out of its migration route. This particular crane was unrecognized at first because it was not native to this region.[8][9]

After the December 15, 1967, collapse of the Silver Bridge and the death of 46 people, the incident gave rise to the legend and connected the Mothman sightings to the bridge collapse. It should be noted that it is not unusual, after the fact, to equate strange happenings to later disasters.

However, there is one encounter that has to rank at the top of the weirdness scale when it comes to Mothman. Most believe that Mothman is a denizen of West Virginia, but Shawnee Harrison, formerly of Zilah, Washington claimed an encounter with Mothman on May 17, 1980. This occurred one-day before Mount St. Helens erupted, killing 57 people and filling the air with millions of tons of heated ash and debris[89].

---

[89] Nunnelly, Barton, *The Inhumanoids: Real Encounters With Beings that Can't Exist*, Triangle Publishing, 2017, Kindle Edition.

Now at the time of her encounter, Shawnee was only five years old. According to her recollection, she watched an amorphous black blob which she later learned as Mothman fly down from a tree to land outside her window. She had been playing alone in her room at the time of the sighting.

According to Shawnee, once Mothman landed, he changed into a human, though his eyes were still black and red. He appeared as a figure that was tall, broad and thick, but still very much human in appearance. He did not speak in the normal manner, but rather spoke to her telepathically. She reported that his mouth never moved during their conversation.

Nothing about the figure was threatening to the five year old. He simply told her to say inside the house, as something bad was gong to happen. As stated above, this was one day before the Mount St. Helen's eruption. The eruption of the volcano covered the house and the orchard with feet of ash. Had she been outside of her house when the eruption occurred, she could have been injured, so this should be viewed as a beneficial occurrence.

She reported that she asked him if he could change into other things beside a man and he proceeded to demonstrate his ability to appear as almost anyone he desired. Finally, he changed into the spiting image of her mother, which was not upsetting apparently until she heard her mother call her name from inside the house. This elicited a panicked scream from the curious five year old.

She reports that when she screamed, the mysterious man smiled at her, changed back into the original amorphous black blob and flew way. Later she came to believe that there was a connection between the creature and the collapsed bridge since she had some relatives who died in the bridge disaster.

FLYING FIGURES

There is report from 1981 concerns an attack by a flying eight-foot tall humanoid with huge leathery wings and a lizard like face. It was reported that this mysterious creature attacked two carloads of adults traveling along a country road in Granite Galls. Granite Falls is located on Mount Philchuck in Washington State.

The witnesses, all in their sixties, reported that they had pulled over to take photographs of the scenery when they saw what they at first thought was a hand glider in the sky. The figure began to descend towards them and they decided that it was time to look at scenery elsewhere, so they loaded into their cards and left the area. To their shock and surprise the entity gave chase and attacked the cars, leaving long scratch marks on both of the vehicles. One of the cars went into the ditch, as the driver was so scared he had a stroke. The other car escaped into town and summoned the police.

In this particular case, apparently the long arm of the law arrived in time to see the perpetrator. According to the reports, the local police arrived in time to shoot at the creature, which was apparently continuing its attack on the damaged automobile in he ditch. Then, being apparently disturbed by their gun battle with the mysterious creature they called in the National Guard. It seems that there have been reports of such creatures in the area going back into the 1940s[90].

HAWKMAN

Sometimes art gives rise to reality and vice versa. No one is sure which came first in this case. In 1986 in Greece three hunters came upon a low flying "man" in the woods sporting a long bird-like beak, leathery skin and lengthy, sharp looking talons. The description given to police by the distraught hunters actually sounded very much like that of Hawkman in the D.C. comic of the same name[91].

FURTHER ATTACKS

In 1986 in Santa Catalina, Brazil, a girl heard the sounds of an altercation coming from outside her house. Naturally curious, she opened the door to see her father fighting with a huge winged entity with triangular shaped eyes, huge black wings, wearing a dark cape and carrying a trident in one human looking hand. Naturally, she was quite shocked and simply froze in fear rather than going to her father's aid.

---

[90] Ibid
[91] Ibid

As she watched her father threw a large piece of wood at his attacker, but the missile literally vanished before it could strike the creature. While we do not know the outcome of this titanic battle, but there are indications that the father and daughter survived the encounter.

Another flying "humanoid" was seen in Kostroma, Russia in 1990. Witnesses at first thought it was some sort of flying machine until it got close enough for them to see it was humanoid. Most witnesses reported that it had large dark wings and no visible neck. It also did not tarry but continued on its mysterious mission.

Then there was also an interesting sighting in 1994 near Mount Rainier, Washington. According to the **Tacoma News Tribune** of May 1, 1994, 18-year old Brian Canfield was driving his pickup truck along a deserted country road leading from the community of Buckley to a small settlement called Camp One when the engine suddenly stopped. His truck came to a screeching halt in the darkness, though his headlights continued to burn brightly, creating a cone of light in front of his truck.

As he sat in his truck considering his options, he made several efforts to restart the vehicle, to no avail. Finally, giving up his efforts to restart the truck, he placed his hand on the door handle and then froze as he saw movement in the cone of light to his front.

At first in the glare of the headlights, he simply saw movement, but then he began to distinguish details. First he saw what he finally realized were huge bird-like feet ending in powerful claws descending from the darkness above the road. Then he saw the legs, the powerful torso and the chest. Then he saw the head and a face that child him to the bone.

The creature's body was covered with blue tinted fur; it had yellowish eyes, tufted ears, sharp looking teeth. He later reported the creature stood at least nine-feet tall and had large black wings that the creature folded against its back. A few minutes later, when the creature spread its wings, they covered the road from side to side.

In interviews, Brian stated that the creature made no threatening moves, it just stood in the middle of the road in front of his truck and stared at him as if puzzled by the truck. Finally, it left as mysteriously as it came and he was left with no doubt that this was a physically powerful creature. When it began to flap is wings to take of, the turbulence that it caused was sufficient to rock his truck. When last seen by Brian, the creature was heading toward Mount Rainier.

BATSQUATCH

Of course, Washington State was not the only place where these flying entities were encountered. In 1993, at Baker's Point, near Allentown, Pennsylvania, hikers encountered a flying entity said to resemble Sasquatch[92]. After a standoff similar to that in Washington State, the creature spread its wings and flew off, vanishing into the sky.

Of course, this was not the first time Batsquatch was encountered by unsuspecting hikers. In 1974, four very experienced hikers in Northern California were stunned to encounter a "thing" that squatted on a rocky ledge some distance above them. It had a grayish color that seemed to blend in with the rocks making it very hard to see.

The creature was described as having a dog-like or a wolf-like face, large feet with talons and the legs, arms and shoulders like that of a man. When it realized it had been seen, the creature spread two big black wings and launched itself form the ledge where it had been sitting into the sky and quickly vanished.

Across the country around Mount Katahdin in Baxter State Park in Maine there are reports of a similar big winged creature said to have the head of a moose. The creature is apparently called the Poomoola and is also known as the Injun Devil.

Of course, no study of this kind would be complete without looking reports on the Internet. From a website known as Riotfest.Org comes reports of flying bat-like humanoids being reported in Chicago in 2017. According to the website, the

---

[92] Nunnelly, Barton, *The Inhumanoids: Real Encounters With Beings that Can't Exist*, Triangle Publishing, 2017, Kindle Edition.

Singular Fortean[93] Society, a website dedicated to investigating the impossible, has recorded over a dozen different sightings of flying humanoids in Chicago so far this year. The most recent was in June of 2017 in Logan Square. A bouncer at a bar called the Owl is said to have seen a bat-like humanoid flying over the lot across the street from the Bar[94].

Chicago is not alone in reporting strange or unusual sightings. Such encounters happen across the country, in act, thee have been similar reports around the world.

Ours is a world of the strange and the unusual, it is just that most of the really odd stories are not reported, as scientists insist that these stories are all just hoaxes. But as you will see, most of these so-called scientists have no idea what they are talking about. Actually there are impossible things happening around us all of the time, but we are so busy with our own lives that we fail to appreciate them.

Let us consider an unusual class of flying creatures, Homo Avis or, in English, birdman. This creature may be responsible for many of the angel reports made by fanatic religious types over the last 2,000 years. As has been pointed out by several followers of Charles Fort and members of the various Fortean Societies, there are actually two creatures that may be responsible for the Homo

---

[93] The Fortean Society was named after Charles Fort a collector of stories of strange occurrence.

[94] Riotfest.org

Avis reports. The stories about the first of these creatures come from the legends of the early Native American Tribes. They talked about a gigantic creature that they called a Thunderbird.

There are many legends about the Thunderbird. The thunderbird is a legendary creature in certain North American indigenous peoples' history and culture. It is considered a supernatural being of power and strength. It is especially important, and frequently depicted, in the art, songs and oral histories of many Pacific Northwest Coast cultures, but is also found in various forms among some peoples of the American Southwest, East Coast of the United States, Great Lakes, and Great Plains.

In Algonquian mythology, the Thunderbird controls the upper world, while the underworld is controlled by the underwater panther or Great Horned Serpent. The thunderbird throws lightning at the underwater creatures and creates thunder by flapping its wings. Thunderbirds in this tradition are commonly depicted as having an X-shaped appearance. This varies between a simple X to recognizable birds. The X-shaped thunderbird is often used to depict the thunderbird with its wings alongside its body and the head facing forwards instead of in profile.

The Menominee of Northern Wisconsin tell of a great mountain that floats in the western sky on which dwell the thunderbirds. They control the rain and hail and delight in fighting and deeds of greatness. They are the enemies of the great horned snakes - the Misikinubik - and have prevented these from overrunning the earth and devouring mankind. They are messengers of the Great Sun himself.

The Ojibwe version of the myth states that the thunderbirds were created by Nanabozho for the purpose of fighting the underwater spirits. They were also used to punish humans who broke moral rules. The thunderbirds lived in the four directions and arrived with the other birds in the springtime. In the fall they migrated south after the ending of the underwater spirits' most dangerous season.

Winnebago tradition states that a man who has a vision of a thunderbird during a solitary fast will become a war chief.

Early European explorers discovered a huge drawing of a Thunderbird on a cliff along the Mississippi. Clearly, the Native Americans knew of some creature that fit the description of what they called the Thunderbird to pain a representation

The next possible culprit for the Homo Avis sightings was, at one time, a living creature. It was known as the Pterodactyl, one of the dinosaurs. Could they still be living today? Well there is a report that a Pterodactyl the size of a goose staggered out of a tunnel in France, shook its wings, and died at the feet of a work crew.

It would also seem that the Pterodactyl may have survived in numerous places around the world as some of the ancient Chinese paintings and statues of dragons bear a remarkable resemblance not only to the Pterodactyl but also the paintings of dragons that came from England and Western Europe. Naturally, since science insists that there was no commerce between the two widely separate areas I ancient times, it would follows that these similar drawings would be proof of the existence of what are called dragons in both of these areas.

The stories that find their ways into the press and into the books on the strange make it clear that we live in a world that is far stranger than we could ever have imagined. This is the first volume in a series entitled "Secrets." Join us as we track down other secrets that hide in the shadows.

INDEX

A

Abgal., 116
Adena, 88
Allen Greg, 107
Annunaki, 37, 39, 72
anthropology, 15
Apocrypha, 31
Archaeology, 13, 15, 17, 22
Arius, 34, 35

B

Batsquatch, 149
Bible, 25, 30, 31, 36, 37, 52, 55, 58, 59, 61, 81, 110, 111, 128
Bonaparte, Napoleon, 129
Book of Genesis, 110
Bureau of Ethnology, 100

C

Caesar Flavius Constantine I, 26
Cahokia Culture, 87, 89
Calalus, 97
Carnarvon, Lord, 13
Carter, Howard, 13
Catalina Museum, 108
Chief Tuscaloosa, 103
Council of Nicea, 27
Count de Saint-Germaine, 59
Craddock, Paul, 76
Cromwell, Oliver, 133, 135, 137

D

De Narvaez, Pablo, 102
de Soto, Hernando, 103, 104
De Vaca, Alvar Nunes Cabeza, 102
Denisovans, 83, 84, 85

E

El Tovar Crystal Canyon, 95
electroplating theory, 77

F

Feder, Kenneth, 22
First Ecumenical Council of the Christian Church, 26
Forester, Brien, 86

G

Gardner, Laurence, 39
German Archaeological Institute in Cairo, 23

H

H. Naledi, 83
Hawass, Zahi, 21, 61, 65, 68
Hawkman, 147
Haze, Xaviant, 91
Herodotus, 14
Hill, Bryan, 91
Hitler, Adolf, 132
Hobbit Race. See Homo floresiensis
Homo Avis, 151, 153
Hopewell, 89, 101
Horomatangi, 116
Hudson, David, 38, 43

I

Icke, David, 95
Indian Mounds, 98, 101
International Forum on New Science, 39

J

Jesus Christ, 27, 29
Joan of Arc, 127
Joseph, Frank, 87, 89

K

Keel, John, 141
Khafra, 22, 23
Khufu, 20, 23
King Charles XII, 131, 132
King Juba of Mauretania, 96
King Nabonidus, 14

L

Lake Okeechobee, 104
Law of Canonicity, 30
Lehner, Mark, 22
Lilith, 118
Lizard People, 119, 120, 121, 123

M

Malone, Walter, 104
Manna, 58
Marble Canyon, 94
Marrs, Jim, 38, 67
Marzulli, L.A, 107, 112, 113
Maussan, Jaime, 112, 113
Methuselah, 37
Michigan Copper, 90
Mississippian culture, 87
monatomic gold. *See* Philosopher's Stone
Moses, 31, 52, 56, 59, 134
Mothman, 141, 142, 144

N

Nicea, 26, 28, 30, 31, 33, 35, 36
Nickell, Joe, 143
NOVA, 21, 22
Nunez, Alvar, 103
Nunnelly, Barton, 115, 127, 129, 144, 149

Nykkjen, 116

O

Oannes, 116, 126
Old Testament, 31
ORME, 39, 55

P

Paracas region of Peru, 86
Pliosaurs, 110
Poomoola, 150
Porphyry, 35
Powell, J.W., 100
Prigg, Mark, 85
Pterodactyls, 110

R

Ranjel, Rodrigo, 103
Red Cave Deer People, 81
reincarnation, 34
Reptilians, 117
Roman Empire, 27, 28, 30, 32, 33, 96

S

Scott, David A., 77
Secundus of Ptolemaid, 34
Septaugint, 31
Serpent People, 118
Sherman, Sherman, 128
Silver Bridge, 141, 142, 144
Silverbell Road artifacts, 97
Sitchin, Zacharia, 37
Socrates, 35
Sphinx, 18, 19, 20, 21, 22, 23, 24, 61, 62, 65
Stadelmann, Rainer, 23
Stone, Elizabeth, 78
Supreme Council of Antiquities, 21, 61

T

Temple of the Moon, 88
Theonas of Marmarica, 34

Theory of Evolution, 80, 84
Thunderbird, 151, 152, 153

U

University of Texas at El Paso (UTEP), 12

W

Washington, George, 128
Watson, Jim, 107
West, John Anthony, 19
Winthrop, John, 99

www.ingramcontent.com/pod-product-compliance
Lightning Source LLC
Chambersburg PA
CBHW071632080526
44588CB00010B/1368